# A
# FIERCE
# HEART

# A FIERCE HEART

## FINDING STRENGTH, COURAGE, AND WISDOM IN ANY MOMENT

## PARALLAX PRESS

BERKELEY, CALIFORNIA

## SPRING WASHAM
### FOREWORD BY JACK KORNFIELD

Parallax Press
P.O. Box 7355
Berkeley, California
94707

parallax.org

Parallax Press is the publishing division of
Plum Village Community of Engaged Buddhism, Inc.

Printed in the United States of America

Cover and text design by Josh Michels
Cover and inset artwork © Paul Lewin
Interior illustrations © Anna Oneglia
Author photo © Nina Omelchenko

"Love after Love" by Derek Walcott is reprinted by permission of the publisher.
"The Dakini Speaks" and "Unconditional" by Jennifer Welwood are included
courtesy of the poet. To purchase Jennifer's collection of spiritual poetry,
*Poems for the Path*, visit jenniferwelwood.com.

ISBN: 978-1-937006-76-1

Library of Congress Cataloging-in-Publication Data

1 2 3 4 / 20 19 18 17

*To the beautiful community at the East Bay Meditation Center.*
*Your strength, courage, and wisdom have inspired me beyond measure.*

# CONTENTS

# FOREWORD

Amidst uncertain times, we need strong and inspiring medicine. In *A Fierce Heart,* you will find this medicine: beautiful teachings and heartfelt stories that can transform your day and change your life. The real purpose of these stories is to awaken and empower you. They will remind you of profound possibilities and provide a sweet, healing balm of wisdom and love for your own difficult and joyful journey.

Told here, Spring's personal tale is also universal. Like the most beloved accounts of sages and shamans, ancient lamas and wise mamas, Spring leads us through the trials and revelations of her own life, to show in intimate and personal ways how the mud we are given can give birth to the lotus.

When you meet her in person, Spring Washam is quite lovable, a fountain of joy and caring laughter. She is a dazzling, big-hearted colleague whom I have known since she was young. She is a passionate activist and teacher who blends depth and dedication.

In this beautiful book, Spring gives you her all. But remember, this girl from Long Beach who became the shaman from the Amazon, the yogi from the Himalayas, is not here to entertain you. She means to challenge you! To insist that as you read, you reflect and inquire as she has done:

What is the calling of your own heart?
How fully are you living your own life, this day, this year?
How free is your spirit, how wide is your compassion?
If you were to be more spiritually adventurous,
what would that mean?
Have you considered meditation? Would more of it
be good for you?
How about shamanic practice, or sacred medicine? Do you
find a calling to it?
Are you called to work for justice, to combine it with
spiritual courage?

Look more deeply, she asks, because doing so opens the gates to joy
and liberation:

Where are you not free?
What limiting beliefs and fears and unhelpful
emotions run your days?
What does your body want to tell you?
What has made you stronger?
What are your deepest and most beautiful intentions
for the years ahead?
What has love taught you?

Something in you knows there is more to life than just following
society's outer focus on money, consumption, and success.

There is a wisdom within you wanting to awaken.
There is a Wise One Who Knows in each of us.
Take time to listen.

Remember, too, honoring the path of awakening is not
a one-time process.
Initiations and openings are demanded in every stage of life.

Amidst the 10,000 joys and sorrows of your human incarnation, at
this time of both miraculous outer development and widespread
injustice, all your courage and wisdom and compassion are needed.

Pause.
Read this book slowly.
Let Spring's stories touch you and enliven you.
And then, follow their inspiration.
Let them lead you on your own miraculous journey.
Many blessings as you go!

—Jack Kornfield
Spirit Rock Meditation Center, 2017

You may encounter many defeats, but you must not be defeated. In fact, it may be necessary to encounter the defeats, so you can know who you are, what you can rise from, how you can still come out of it.

**—MAYA ANGELOU**

## CHAPTER ONE

# BLOOMING IN THE MUD

MY VERY FIRST MEMORY is a happy one. My sister and I are sitting on the kitchen counter looking down into our small, rusty toaster. It's a Saturday morning, and we're watching cartoons and eating cinnamon toast. For a three-year-old, it doesn't get much better than this. When the toast finally pops, I smother it in butter, sugar, and cinnamon, then joyfully leap back onto our old, green couch. I was so young then, I could never have imagined the twists and turns my life would have in store.

I came into the world on December 26, 1973, at St. Mary's County Hospital in Long Beach, California. My birth was not the celebrated, magical moment we all hope for. It was the opposite. My parents' relationship, which had always been rocky, completely unraveled during my mother's pregnancy with me. A couple of days after I was born, we moved into a tiny apartment in a large housing complex in Bellflower, California, a low-income neighborhood between east Long Beach and Compton. We were surrounded by gang violence, gunshots, sirens, and helicopters buzzing all night long. My father was in and out of the house during my first three years, and then one day he was gone. Even though I was so young, I was aware of the tension and stress in the air. By the time I was five, I remember thinking, "This is gonna be a tough life." As a child, my heart reached out for my mother and even for my absent father, but instinctively I knew they were just wounded children themselves and I was on my own.

My parents met in Long Beach in the late 1960s while sleeping in the living room of a mutual friend named Billie, a prostitute and drug dealer who, my mother said, had a beautiful heart. When they met, my mother had just left her first husband, whom she'd married in Tijuana at age sixteen, and my father had just gotten out of prison after serving a year for check forgery. They were young, homeless, and completely down on their luck. Neither had family and both were looking for someone or someplace to call home.

Within days, they'd fallen head over heels in love. Desperate to bury their pasts, they took off in an old Cadillac to start a new life together. Like so many of their generation, they were also searching for meaning and simply wanted to be happy and free. My father had a longing to study meditation and Eastern philosophy, and their road trip was meant to be a great spiritual adventure.

But their Cadillac broke down in Reno and, on an impulse, they decided to get married there. My father was a dark-skinned African American, and my mother is of European ancestry. Interracial couples were very controversial in the late sixties and they had a hard time finding a minister who would even talk to them, let alone marry them. Finally, they were married in a tiny Nevada chapel, and from that day on they were subjected to hatred and racism almost every single day of their relationship.

Neither of them had had much formal education, and their lack of steady employment and access to affordable housing kept them on the move constantly. It was one big disappointment after another, and the initial joy they once shared unraveled into years of pain. The constant struggle of their lives began to take a toll on the relationship, and the happiness they'd briefly shared was replaced by mistrust, accusations, and constant fighting. They wanted to put their past behind them, but the traumas they'd suffered growing up just kept haunting them.

As children, they'd both endured extreme neglect and severe physical abuse by their fathers. Their violent upbringings mirrored each other's almost exactly. In an attempt to salvage their fragile marriage and create something beautiful, my mother was convinced she needed to have children. She longed for the loving family she'd never had. My father already had two kids: one had died tragically and the other he hadn't seen in years. Despite his plea not to have more children, my sister arrived first and I came shortly after. That didn't bring my parents closer; in fact, the tension between them mounted.

My father became increasingly erratic and unstable, and he spent nights partying and sleeping with other women. They both got lost in addictions, my mother to food and my father to drugs, money, and life on the street. He would disappear for days at a time, eventually months, and my mother was left alone to fend for herself. She worked as much as she could and, with Medi-Cal and food stamps, we got by. By the time I was born, my father had pretty much abandoned the family, leaving us penniless, vulnerable, and on our own.

During years of traveling around the world and teaching mindfulness meditation, I've heard hundreds of unbelievable stories of individuals facing adversity that have opened my heart and given me faith and courage. I am particularly drawn to stories of people who overcome pain and trauma to create beauty and end up helping others. It's not where we start that defines us; it's where we end up that transforms a good story into a brilliant one. The challenges we face in the beginning become the gifts that inspire the ending. Those who overcome great suffering in pursuit of personal freedom provide us with the inspiration we need to meet our own challenges with strength, courage, and wisdom.

I've collected many moving biographies—accounts of Tibetan and Indian yogis, mystics, hermits, musicians, shamans, activists, artists, clergy, and masters from many spiritual traditions—and I'm constantly reminded of the strength of the human spirit to soar, even in the darkest situations. Our narratives are the stories of ourselves and of our people. Some of us are the descendants of slaves and others have fled war-torn countries with nothing. Some grew up in wealthy families that looked perfect on the outside, but were filled with violence, abuse, and confusion within. Some of us are from middle- and working-class backgrounds, and have not yet looked deeply into the causes of our suffering. There's never a need for shame about who you are or where you come from. Learning to embrace your history, identity, and ancestry is an important step in the process of healing and growing. When we reflect on our own stories, it can feel like we'll be stuck in the mud forever, but this never has to be the case.

If you were to write your own autobiography, it would be filled with triumphs and tragedies, laughter and tears. Each of us has stories of how we came to be the person we are today. Although our circumstances are unique and our backgrounds diverse, the threads of all our journeys can be woven together into a beautiful, integrated tapestry.

I compare my life to that of a lotus flower, which can bloom for a thousand years in the muddiest of waters. The unfolding petals of the lotus represent the awakening of the heart. At the age of five I had the thought, "This is gonna be a tough life." But how else does one learn to bloom in the mud? I can now look back with the eyes of wisdom and see the perfection in everything that has happened. I needed all of it, every ounce of mud, in order to bloom. Part of the beauty and mystery of life is that we are in a continuous state of growth, very much like the lotus flower. The Buddha said that in a human life, we experience ten thousand joys and ten thousand sorrows. None of us is free from either.

Cultivating a fierce heart is about learning to embrace it all, even the most painful aspects of our lives—every experience and all of ourselves. We have to open up to *everything* in order to transform it. We become willing to use every condition, challenge, and misery as a teaching, no matter how bad it feels or how dark it gets. Some of the wisest and most courageous people I know have also bloomed in mud. When we allow the shadows and the suffering in, they become the vehicles for our healing. Heartbreak, loss, and the worst betrayals become the fuel for transformation.

We can learn how to use the mud and muck of our lives to wake up and grow. When it feels impossible, that is exactly the time when we need a fierce heart the most. Let it *all* burn in the cosmic fires, so you can forge your fierceness and grow stronger and wiser. No matter what you've been through, *now* is the starting point, so if you're feeling hopeless or at a loss, please trust me when I say your greatest moments are yet to come.

There are only two mistakes one can make along the road to truth; not going all the way and not starting.

**—ANONYMOUS**

## CHAPTER TWO

# ANSWERING THE CALL

THERE COMES A TIME IN LIFE when you hear the Great Calling. This archetypal theme appears in stories, fairy tales, movies, and the great myths from around the world. It appears in the lives of awakened beings, including the Buddha, Jesus, and countless others throughout space and time. When we hear this inner voice, it is our summons, a holy message that we're at a crossroads and a new chapter of life is about to begin.

The Great Calling is an invitation to adventure. It's the yellow brick road beckoning us on to a higher path. When we respond to the calling, it becomes a powerful force for change that unlocks ancestral memories. We go inside ourselves and reflect on who we are and why we are here. If you can feel this calling of your heart, it will guide you like a GPS system helping you navigate the long road home.

Prince Siddhartha Gautama was born under a host of favorable signs in India, 2600 years ago. His father, a wealthy king, was intent on grooming his son to be his successor, but when Siddhartha was just a few days old, a wise sage proclaimed that the prince would become a world-renowned spiritual teacher.

Siddhartha grew up having a privileged life, with every imaginable luxury and opportunity you could imagine. He excelled in the arts, philosophy, and sports. He married a beautiful princess, had a handsome son, and lived pleasurably within the walls of his father's grand palace. But when he was twenty-nine years old, Siddhartha felt a deep dissatisfaction in his heart. He was tired of being walled up, even in a palace, and longed to explore the world around him.

After countless requests to see the countryside, Siddhartha's overprotective father finally relented and let him visit a nearby park. Upon hearing the news, the gods and spirits arranged for the prince to encounter a series of signs designed to get his attention and show him his true path in life. These signs are known as the Four Heavenly Messengers.

The first messenger was an elderly man, covered in wrinkles, bent over, and barely able to walk. Siddhartha's father had only allowed beautiful, young servants in the palace, and the sight of the old man frightened the prince. He realized that his youth would end some day and he too would grow old.

The second heavenly messenger was a sick man, covered in bloody sores and writhing in pain while lying on the floor of a mud hut. Siddhartha felt profoundly sad and sat helplessly beside him. The king had forbidden those who were ill from entering the palace, and Siddhartha had no prior experience of illness. When he realized that everyone becomes sick, his heart grew heavy.

The third heavenly messenger was the most shocking of all. Siddhartha encountered death for the first time. As he wandered through a small village, Siddhartha came upon a funeral procession. A body wrapped in cloth was being carried to the charnel ground for cremation. Siddhartha watched the deceased's family

Don't shut down the process. Drowning out the voices that are trying to get our attention won't work either. The highest part of ourselves will keep knocking on our door, saying, *"Now* is the time to enter the path. It's why you are here. Remember who you are." The Great Calling is the first stage of the spiritual path, an archetypal shift. It's the one call you have to take. It's lifesaving. Bow to the wisdom of the ancestors and trust the divine intelligence that's guiding the process.

When you say yes to the call, the people, situations, and opportunities you need to move forward will present themselves at the perfect moment. A thousand invisible hands magically open, each offering you loving support. You might find refuge in a spiritual teacher or set of teachings. Synchronicities may appear through books, images, YouTube videos, and messages from friends. You're thinking about going to Egypt, and someone shows up at your house with a book on Egypt. Or you're thinking of quitting your job, and you keep running into people everywhere who have just quit their jobs. Spirits are watching over you. The universe is revealing itself through you.

You may be guided to go on a vision quest or visit holy sites that hold power and meaning for you. You may have visions, dreams, or even experiences of non-ordinary states of consciousness. Look around and notice that there are signs and symbols everywhere, all signaling that something important is happening. The Earth herself is your guide, encouraging your effort to wake up and live with more freedom. Sacred objects, animals, rocks, crystals, and other items may appear in unexpected ways. All are part of the Great Calling, signs that something important is happening.

The Great Calling can be a time of prayer as we learn to listen to the guidance of a higher power. I have heard of a Lakota elder quote that says: "There is the world of the flesh and the spirit world; when the flesh is gone, the spirits remain, forever, their voices speak to those who listen." We might call this God, the Great Spirit, Universal Love, the Creator, Christ consciousness, Wakan Tanka, Buddha Nature, Primordial Light, the Force, Innate Compassion, Gaia, Non-Localized Consciousness, or the Field. All these terms refer to a source calling us home, the jewel in the heart of the lotus. It's time for us to bloom.

In 1997, my mother's partner inadvertently left a book about meditation on my dining room table. Beautifully written by a Hindu teacher, it was a "heavenly message," reminding me of my life's purpose. I felt, for the first time in years, this incredibly strong desire to live a spiritually-based life. Then I forgot about it. I moved into a tiny run-down house in the worst section of East Oakland with a new boyfriend I hardly knew. We were definitely in the 'hood, and everyone seemed to be in a bad mood. Even our dog was grumpy all the time.

My boyfriend and I argued about pretty much everything. We worked together at a timeshare company, talking people into buying expensive Palm Springs timeshares they didn't need and, in most cases, couldn't afford. I was thousands of dollars in debt and was being hounded by creditors twenty-four hours a day. I was becoming increasingly erratic, feeling depressed, and angry about the direction my life was taking. I was living with a man who made me miserable and doing a job I couldn't stand. I was overwhelmed by anxiety and a sense of desperation and couldn't stop crying. I began smoking a lot of marijuana to numb the pain, but drugs and alcohol were, at best, only a temporary solution. Then, in the course of one day, I got fired from my job for calling in sick, my tortured relationship began collapsing, and the Oakland Honda dealership called to repossess my car. As everything fell apart, I lay on the couch eating cookies, praying to God for help, and crying for a week straight.

Miraculously, I heard about a ten-day Buddhist meditation retreat that would be starting in a few weeks in Southern California. This was it, the break I'd been waiting for! I was truly desperate.

I had been meditating on my own, but I knew I needed a real teacher and a community for support. I was so excited by the idea of having ten days of silence, healthy food, and proper meditation instruction, I was willing to do anything to get there. Somehow I got the money together and registered.

On the day the retreat was going to start, I made the nine-hour drive from Oakland to the Southern California desert, crying hysterically, chain-smoking cigarettes, and drinking Diet Mountain Dew by the gallon. My boyfriend and I had had an extremely dramatic final break up the night before and I had all my belongings in the car, my last $25, and nowhere to go after the retreat was over. I didn't care; I *knew* if I could just get myself to the retreat, everything would make sense.

Looking back, I see that what I experienced during those ten days in the desert was a genuine awakening experience. It's not easy to explain. I spent hours in sitting meditation, and my screaming, tormented mind finally got silent and peaceful. During walking meditation, I released oceans of tears with each step. For the first time, I encountered the teachings of the Buddha and immediately knew I'd found my path. I met my beautiful teacher, Jack Kornfield, whose loving encouragement and steadfast belief in me have helped transform my life. In the profound stillness and silence, I was finally able to understand myself.

On the last day of the retreat, I hiked way out into the desert and up on top of a small hill, where I prayed and made a vow to myself to follow these teachings "until the very end."

This, my friends, was the beginning of my meditation path. It wasn't the prettiest of starts. Beginnings often aren't. After that first retreat in the desert, I went on to do many more retreats, spending a thousand days in silent retreat over the next twenty years. I answered the call, I keep answering it… and what a ride it continues to be.

"The Journey" by Mary Oliver

One day you finally knew
what you had to do, and began,
though the voices around you
kept shouting
their bad advice—
though the whole house
began to tremble
and you felt the old tug
at your ankles.
"Mend my life!"
each voice cried.
But you didn't stop.
You knew what you had to do,
though the wind pried
with its stiff fingers
at the very foundations—
though their melancholy
was terrible.
It was already late
enough, and a wild night,
and the road full of fallen
branches and stones.
But little by little,
as you left their voices behind,
the stars began to burn
through the sheets of clouds,
and there was a new voice,
which you slowly
recognized as your own,
that kept you company

as you strode deeper and deeper
into the world,
determined to do
the only thing you could do—
determined to save
the only life you could save.[1]

For a long time I had been my own stranger, but everything I went through in learning how to accept myself brought me to the doorsteps of dharma, the Buddhist path.

**—JARVIS JAY MASTERS**

## CHAPTER THREE

# PRISON OF THE MIND

AT LEAST ONCE A WEEK, as I travel between teaching at Spirit Rock in Woodacre and teaching at East Bay Meditation Center in Oakland, I drive past San Quentin, the oldest prison in California and one of the nation's most infamous. Jarvis Jay Masters is one of the 734 men currently living there on death row. He's been incarcerated since 1981 and on death row since 1990. Jarvis has spent the majority of his life locked in a tiny cell in the maximum security unit. He has few privileges and is allowed out of his cell only a few hours a week.

Jarvis's story is a tale of violence and loss, as well as compassion and the awakening of the heart. He grew up in an abusive home, and both his parents were drug addicts. His family split up when Jarvis was nine, and he and his siblings entered the foster-care system, moving from place to place and experiencing abuse and neglect by foster care homeworkers and foster families. At the age of twelve, he became a ward of the court and, along with many other African American boys, was under the jurisdiction of the California Youth Authority (CYA), which houses the state's most serious youth offenders.

CYA is known to be violent and punitive. When he was released at age seventeen, Jarvis went on a crime spree, robbing a string of stores and restaurants. No one was physically hurt, but he was arrested and entered San Quentin when he was still a teenager. Young, alone, and afraid, Jarvis had few options for surviving except to join a prison gang.

A few years into his sentence, a guard was stabbed to death, and he and two other men were charged with the crime. Although Jarvis was locked in his cell at the time of the murder, he was accused of sharpening the weapon that was used to stab the guard and, in one of the longest trials in California history, he was given the death penalty. He has always denied participating in the crime, but sadly his pleas of innocence had no effect on the verdict. He has spent the last twenty-six years waiting to be executed, while simultaneously appealing his case.

During Jarvis's trial, his attorney sent him books on meditation and, to everyone's surprise, he read them. He felt he had nothing to lose and time on his hands, so he began to practice meditation. Jarvis quickly realized that he had a passion for the teachings of the Buddha and began spending hours a day on the floor of his cell meditating. Within a couple of years, he began to transform his mind and his prison experience. A place that had felt unbearable became his sanctuary. From the confines of death row, his deepening understanding of Buddhism and his loving heart caught the attention of Chagdud Tulku Rinpoche, a great Tibetan master. Rinpoche visited him and became his main teacher. Other well-known teachers began visiting as well, offering Jarvis *bodhisattva* vows,[1] teachings, and blessings.

Inspired by his transformation, a team of legal, spiritual, and emotional advisors grew around Jarvis. He was encouraged to write about his experiences and the challenges of living a spiritual life as a death row inmate. Miraculously, he was able to publish two books, and his heartfelt stories have touched the lives of thousands, including Archbishop Desmond Tutu, death-penalty abolitionist Sister Helen Prejean, and activist professor Angela Davis. A transformed human being, Jarvis has become a powerful advocate of nonviolence in San Quentin and beyond. Through practicing meditation and observing his mind, he discovered a happiness that is no longer dependent on outer conditions. The state of California may choose to execute Jarvis or keep him locked up forever, but for him the outcome will not change the peace of mind he now possesses. He has found a profound inner freedom that no one can take away.

The prison-industrial complex has always been a part of my life. From a spiritual perspective, we can view prison as a symbol, a representation of oppression, power, and control. My father spent time in prison in his early twenties and it changed him. It was there that he recognized how important freedom is, and he promised himself never to go back. He was able to keep that vow. Sadly, my little brother Roman has had the opposite experience. He began going to jail when he was fourteen. Guns, drugs, and theft were things that always drew him in. I remember visiting him in juvenile hall, when he would promise me he was going to change his life. As soon as he would get released, he would fall back into the same trap over and over. We had a sweet reunion several years ago when he was released after serving five long years in an adult correctional facility on the East Coast. His experiences were brutal and inhumane. He was often locked in solitary confinement for months at a time. The whole family rallied around him to help him begin a new life. We were all so hopeful. I showered him with all my love and support, but it just wasn't enough. In spite of being smart, handsome, and committed to change, within six weeks of being released he was involved in another violent crime and this time was given a ten-year prison sentence. My brother and I have always had a special bond and when I received the news, it broke my heart. Yet I believe one day he will find the keys to freedom.

Some of us aren't locked up in physical prisons, but still we know what it feels like to feel confined and crazy. I always used to feel claustrophobic, like a lion stuck in a cage, trapped in my mind. As a teenager, I began studying psychology in order to understand my mind. At eighteen, I was so depressed that I was willing to try anything to feel better. This led me to my first teacher, Michael Bernard Beckwith, the founder of Agape International Spiritual Center in Culver City, California. Agape was my first spiritual home and the teachings I received there changed the course of my life.

When we finally muster the courage to look inside, we discover that we are living in a prison constructed by our own mind. Until we start to pay attention, we're all just doing time. I am deeply inspired by Jarvis because he discovered that the real prisons are the *inner* ones. While living on death row, he has had to search *inside* for joy, truth, and beauty, to discover his own happiness. To free ourselves, we have to unlock the doors *from the inside*. The keys are within us. We need a fierce heart and the willingness to face ourselves.

Sometimes, we feel imprisoned by our family, our culture, our addictions, our relationships, even our bodies—due to disability, illness, or even our appearance. I felt imprisoned by a deep depression and self-hatred, never feeling *good enough*. I would spend hours every day wishing that I were different, that I were smarter, that I would have more friends, more money, or a different family. I wondered if I would ever be happy. Worst of all is the deeply held belief that there's no release and no escape.

In one retelling of a Hopi myth, the Creator gathers all of creation and says, "I want to hide something from the humans until they're ready for it. It is the realization that they create their own reality. The eagle says, "Give it to me. I will take it to the moon." The Creator says, "No, one day they will go there and find it." The salmon says, "I will bury it at the bottom of the oceans." The Creator says, "No, they will go there too." The buffalo says, "I will bury it out on the great plains." The Creator says, "No, they will cut into the skin of the earth and find it even there." Grandmother Mole, who lives in the breast of Mother Earth and has no physical eyes but sees with spiritual eyes, says, "Put it inside of them." And the Creator says, "It is done."

The Buddha once began a Dharma talk by asking, "The whole world is in a tangle—inner tangles and outer tangles. Who can untangle the great tangle?"[2] The cruelest prison wardens are the ones in our heads. They abuse us the most. With our thoughts, the Buddha observed, we create the world. Science confirms that our thinking affects every aspect of our lives. Since the prison we're confined in is built by our own thoughts, emotions, and beliefs, the keys to freedom are in our hands. We can stay locked up, or we can look within and learn to unlock the door.

The ultimate goal of the spiritual path is to uncover the ways we imprison ourselves, to realize that this elaborate system of thinking and behaving is constructed by our own mind. We cling to beliefs— family belief systems, national and cultural ideologies, ideas we've formed or that others have told us—about who we are. Most of our stories begin with, "I am a bad person because…," and you can fill in the blank. Every tale you have about yourself is made up. Some are epic fantasies and some are dark dramas filled with pain and suffering. In either case, we're prisoners of our own thought forms. We think thousands of thoughts every day. Most are variations of the thoughts we had yesterday and will have tomorrow. One moment you experience peace, the next moment you're in hell, all because a thought has passed through your mind. Who would you be without your story? Imagine that for a moment. There is a Chinese proverb:

*Watch your thoughts, they become words;*
*watch your words, they become actions;*
*watch your actions, they become habits;*
*watch your habits, they become character;*
*watch your character, for it becomes your destiny.*

The mind spins all day long, generating one story after another. When we believe our painful thoughts, dark emotions follow, and a four-alarm fire is triggered. No wonder we feel so much stress— we're constantly reacting to the nightmarish movies that are playing over and over in our heads. We're addicted to these dramas. To have peace, we need to break the addiction to our destructive thinking. To get out of prison, we have to become mindful of our thoughts and begin unlinking the chains of suffering. We have the power to do this.

Years ago, I dreamed I was at a carnival where there were dozens and dozens of rides, food stands, games, and freak sideshows. It was nighttime, and there were thousands of colorful, flashing lights. Crazy carnival music was blaring out of the loudspeakers, and it was impossible to hear anything else or even think straight. The moment I entered the carnival grounds, I was surrounded by a large group of insane-looking clowns who kept pushing me onto different rides, laughing hysterically, and screaming insults in my face. This went on for what seemed like hours, and with each passing moment, things got moving faster and faster. I felt nauseated from the rides, the noise, and the screaming clowns, and started crying and begging them to stop and let me go. All I could think of was how to get out of there, and I began feeling more and more desperate.

At that moment on the far side of the circus, I spotted a tiny door with a small green neon exit sign. I leaped up and down and shouted, "That's it! I want to leave! I see the exit." At that moment, the entire carnival froze and became completely silent. The head clown brought his giant red nose directly down to mine and screamed, "Leave? Nobody ever wants to leave! Leave then! Fine, go ahead, leave!" That was all the encouragement I needed, and as I sprinted toward the exit, the deafening sound of the carnival returned. As I put my hand on the doorknob, I understood this was a rare opportunity to escape that hellish environment.

Bob Marley sang, "Emancipate yourselves from mental slavery; none but ourselves can free our minds."[3] Thoughts are not reality; to see this we have to slow down and look carefully. It's not easy to see, but true freedom lies beneath the stories. You can sit here and make up a story of heaven or hell, and then live in one or the other. Our whole world is doing this and it has reached epidemic proportions. Stories of greed, hatred, and delusion are everywhere. No one is questioning their own mind; they are just reacting. Either way, the story is *a thought*. It's not happening now. Before I received instruction in meditation, I believed every thought and every painful story that came to mind. These dramas only have power if we believe them.

After my clown dream, I decided to stop blaming others for my unhappiness and to find the exit myself. When I relied on others to make me happy, I was simply redecorating my prison cell. When my new boyfriend drove me crazy and the party ended, I was back in my cell, alone again. Sometimes I would be in a nice environment with everything I wanted, and I was still unhappy! Then I discovered that others feel their own version of this same suffering, and I became determined to find the keys. The intensity of my pain, the fear, rage, and grief of being trapped led me to meditation. Freedom can only be found within. When I stopped focusing on external causes and began looking at my own mind, a shift occurred.

Rumi tells the story of a man who is crawling on the ground beneath an oil street lamp. It was the thirteenth century in Persia, but this could be anyplace today. A friend asks what he's doing, and he says, "I'm looking for my key." So the friend helps him search. They look everywhere, and an hour later they still haven't found it. The friend asks, "Are you sure you lost your key here?" "No," the man replies, "I lost it in my house." "Then why are you looking here?" "Because the light is here." We are so like this. It's time to start looking for our keys where they are, where we left them.

In a *Peanuts* cartoon, Charlie Brown sits down at Lucy's advice booth and begins telling her about all his pain and suffering. Lucy cuts him off, saying, "Chuck! The problem with you is *you*," and she extends her hand for the five-cent payment. Charlie Brown pays her and then shouts, "That's not a real answer!" and Lucy responds, "I just point out the problem, Chuck. I don't give answers." Charlie wanders away more unsteady and disheartened than before. But Lucy's advice is true—the problem *is* us. This is good news. When we know this, we have a path forward.

Spiritual teachers from every time and tradition have left us road maps to follow and keys to unlock our prison doors. The Buddha called his teaching the *Dharma*, a set of principles and practices we practice in order to untangle our confusion. It is the way to step off the wheel of suffering and enter the path to freedom. These teachings destroy the prisons within our mind. Just as athletes and musicians have to train, we need to *practice* meditation and mindfulness so that we can learn to focus our mind and open the doors to freedom. It's our insanity that we are leaving behind and everything we need to accomplish this is within.

If I climb to the top of a ladder, I might discover a world I never knew existed, but I can take only a glimpse. With a glimpse of freedom, we see the key, but are we ready to open the door? Allowing in the new might mean to die to our old way of being, to habits we formed to protect ourselves but that now imprison us. It's not easy to say goodbye to our familiar cell. We've decorated it and in some way we feel comfortable there, even though it's painful. Walking through the door and leaving the known world behind can be difficult. We need faith, the willingness to live in the unknown for a while. But the real question is, "Do I really want to be free?"

No one saves us but ourselves. No one can and no one may.
We ourselves must walk the path.

**—THE BUDDHA**

## CHAPTER FOUR

# SCHOOL OF LIFE

THE SCHOOL OF LIFE is always in session. In my heart I know without a doubt that every encounter, experience, thought, feeling, and relationship is an opportunity to learn. We can grow equally from both the beautiful and the difficult experiences. The School of Life teaches us to use everything, even the most horrific and terrifying situations, to learn about ourselves. Every experience is a mirror reflecting parts of ourselves back to us. Living this way is a fast track toward ending our pain and confusion. It's a radical approach because we flip the script upside down and learn to embrace the difficult instead of run from it.

The Sufi poet Hafiz writes, "You carry all the ingredients to turn your life into a nightmare—Don't mix them!"[1] You carry all the ingredients to turn your existence into joy—Mix them, mix them! In order to learn to mix the ingredients of our lives wisely, we have to understand how things work. We have to open to it all and plant the seeds that we want to grow. We tend to think that what is fun and pleasurable is good and what is painful and difficult is bad. However, if you begin to view your life as a classroom you, will discover a much deeper truth.

In the midst of a painful experience, it's hard to imagine this very suffering is our ally, encouraging us toward growth and insight. But on reflection, we see how much we're able to learn about ourselves and our patterns from challenging situations. Whenever I feel hurt or triggered, I get down on my knees and ask to see the lesson. What is this painful situation showing me? I want to understand what teaching is here. When I inquire with sincere interest in knowing, things that have been hidden reveal themselves and circumstances change. Instead of feeling victimized, I see what I didn't know before. I open my heart and trust in the curriculum of the School of Life.

A few years ago I had the chance to live in the Peruvian jungle for a year and study plants and the shamanic traditions. I decided to take a break for a few weeks and go up to a sacred valley and visit the mountains. I went to Cusco, a city in the Peruvian Andes, which was once the capital of the Inca Empire. It sits at an altitude of over 11,000 feet and the majestic mountains are alive with spirit. I decided to join a group of people to go on a hike and explore the mountains a bit. I arrived at our meeting spot at eight o'clock in the morning and was immediately disappointed. I'd thought I was going with an elder Andean shaman, but his two young apprentices showed up instead. Juan and Miguel seemed way too young and immature, so I didn't feel much of a heart connection with either of them. After collecting some supplies, we took an hour-long bus ride out into the middle of nowhere. To my great shock, they pointed to a large mountain in the distance and said, "We're going to climb that!" As we got going, I was getting more and more exhausted and I couldn't seem to catch my breath. My head started pounding from the high altitude and I was getting burned in the scorching sun. The two apprentices showed no signs of turning back and they didn't have much compassion when I told them I was feeling very sick. They just kept saying, "You can do it," while laughing.

This was turning out to be one of the worst days of my life. The other members of our small group seemed fine; but I wasn't. After many hours I started to get angry. I asked them to please take me back. I was in serious pain and getting dizzier with each step. My head was pounding, I felt nauseated, I couldn't breathe properly, and I was literally foaming at the mouth! They just laughed and kept walking forward, full of energy. Finally we reached the scariest part at the base of the mountain, it was straight up hill from there. As hard as I tried, I couldn't do it. My cheap tennis shoes were slipping on the long, slick blades of grass and huge gusts of wind were causing me to fall backward. In my eyes, the whole situation was becoming extremely dangerous. Finally, halfway up the mountainside, I screamed that I couldn't go on and I demanded they take me home. I sat down and began to argue with Juan and Miguel. They kept asking me why I couldn't do it, which infuriated me. Then I completely lost myself and started screaming, *"I can't do it!"* A giant gust of wind came up and I held on to the mountainside for dear life. Then I spontaneously started sobbing. As I cried, I started to listen to myself scream, "I can't do it" over and over. In reality, that had been a familiar mantra throughout my life, this deeply held belief that I couldn't do things. Old memories began playing in my mind while I screamed and wailed, hanging on to the side of the mountain. The guides just sat down and stared at me curiously. I think for the first time they realized that I was battling something very powerful within myself. They stopped laughing and started praying. As I shrieked hysterically and pounded my fist on the earth, Juan and Miguel finally began acting like shamans. They began singing, chanting, and offering tobacco prayers to the mountain spirits. After some time, my crying stopped. I stood up, collected myself, and silently climbed effortlessly to the top of the mountain.

Later that evening when I returned home to the tiny cottage where I was staying, my back went out in excruciating pain. My body was sunburned and I felt like I had been in a battle. As I lay in bed, recovering over the next two days, I began to realize how important that day had been. I saw how strong I was. I saw that I underestimated myself all the time. I wouldn't want to repeat a day like that, but I learned something very valuable. I look back now and it makes me laugh! What a lesson!

Nobody wants to deal with difficulties and pain. However, I am the first to admit that when I review my life, I can honestly say it was during the darkest times that I grew the most. As students, we have to study *all* our experiences and see the patterns of our craziness, and we will also see strength, courage, and compassion we didn't realize we had. We learn who we are, what we can tolerate, and what we cannot. When things are hard and challenging, it forces us to face things in a different way. We learn forgiveness, surrender, and letting go. We discover our backbone and begin to access a spiritual power we had no idea was there. Our suffering becomes the sacred compost that helps us grow. Thomas Merton put it this way, "Prayer and love are learned in the hour when prayer becomes impossible and the heart has turned to stone."[2]

My Tibetan Buddhist teachers have inspired me so much over the years. They have told me stories from the old days about how they would pray for difficulties in order to develop more courage and patience. What we usually perceive as obstacles are always essential steps on the path. When we have childhood suffering or we experience the death of a loved one, a betrayal, or the loss of everything, it's difficult to appreciate how it might serve us. So we have to ask, "What can I learn from this?" and then sit quietly and listen. Allow the answers to arise slowly from within. If we've been fortunate to meet the teachings and receive guidance in the practice, we may see that through asking and waiting, we can come to trust the loving intelligence that guides all life. With a fierce heart and the practice of faith and trust, you discover that life isn't happening *to* you, it's happening *for* you. Sometimes when I'm really quiet, I can hear a sound like the beat of a drum, and it reminds me to pay attention, to listen, to wake up. We are human beings living in a world with beauty and tragedy, suffering and freedom. To be alive means that we will experience it all.

I'd like to share the courageous story of my friend Atira, who recovered from cancer after a long process. While not everyone with cancer should adopt her approach, I offer her example to show the importance of hope in even the most hopeless situations in the School of Life.

## ATIRA'S STORY

Exactly ten years ago, I was diagnosed with cervical cancer. I still remember the shock that rippled through my cells as the doctor revealed the diagnosis over the phone. I was a healthy young woman who ate well, exercised, kept to a vegetarian diet, didn't even drink coffee, meditated and did yoga every day, and followed my passion and purpose in life. How could I have cancer? At that time, I was working as a creative art therapist with child refugees in one of the refugee camps along the Thailand-Burma border. Little did I know that this diagnosis was one of the most powerful and profound initiations of my life. Over the phone, my Thai doctor persuaded me that an operation was the best choice and I had to go immediately into surgery. Shocked, devastated, and isolated, within a week, I had packed up my little forest home in the jungle, said goodbye to my beloved clients, and headed to Bangkok for surgery. After a very intrusive and traumatic surgical procedure, the doctor shared another diagnosis—that unfortunately the cancer had spread and I needed to go for chemotherapy. Another wave of shock rippled through my being. This time, I met it with the resolve that there was no way I would go through the medical system again, and that I would find my own way of noninvasive healing. This deep and powerful inner voice told me implicitly that I was the master of my own healing journey, that the cancer could be cured by the power of my mind, heart, and spirit. So I said to the doctor, no thanks. I resolved to focus on my healing and recovery. This illness was a doorway, a threshold to cracked open the seed of my understanding, my connection as a woman to my beautiful body, to healing my ancient ancestral feminine wounds, to understanding, loving, and respecting myself, my cycles, my sexuality, me being a woman, and more. It changed my life forever. It is one of the biggest gifts that life has given to me. This process reminded me of the potent poem by the poet Kahlil Gibran: "Your pain is the breaking of the shell that encloses your understanding…"[3] After my discharge from the hospital, I moved to a healing community in northeast Thailand, and stayed there for eight months, where I dedicated every moment of my life to healing and understanding my illness and why it was there. I immersed myself in every teaching I could find on women's reproductive health. I prayed, meditated, laughed, wept an ocean of tears, healed, unearthed my shadows, released, danced, created art, practiced yoga, changed my diet, and discovered and channeled deep feminine meditations and ways of intuitively healing my cells and my female ancestry until, at the end of eight months, I was so connected to my body that I knew intrinsically and intuitively that my cancer had gone. My higher self was right. I am my own master, and I have the power to heal myself. That month, I went back to Bangkok to check with my doctor, and I was right. The cancer cells had gone and they have never returned. Now, ten years later, I have never felt better.

The School of Life is not linear. It's not just first grade followed by second grade and then third grade. The School of Life operates in spirals and circles. The lessons cycle around again and again until we get the message and pass that course. It can feel frustrating, like the movie *Groundhog Day*, as though we're reliving the same painful relationships, addictions, and traumas over and over again. The cycles repeat for years, even lifetimes. The Buddha asked his monks, "Which is greater, the water in the ocean or the tears you've shed while wandering in *samsara?*"[4] Then he answered his own question: "The tears." We shed an ocean of tears until we wake up.

If you walk into any high school in the US, the students sitting in the front of the classroom are usually well prepared. They have their pens out, their homework ready, and are able to answer every question. Teachers usually love the students in the front rows. As you begin to move back row by row, the students are less and less engaged. Finally, as you reach the back row, it's not a pretty sight. Those in the back tend to be completely checked out or asleep, and it's likely they will have to repeat the class.

One definition of insanity is to do the same thing over and over, each time expecting a different result. The Buddhist word for this repetitive pattern is *samsara*, "endless wandering." We are lost, looking for happiness while repeating the things that lead to unhappiness. Life goes round and round, like a hamster on a wheel. "Didn't I just date this exact same guy? Wasn't my last job just like this one?" Things repeat until we get the lesson. It's not just about who we're dating or where we're working. The constant is *us*. Wherever we go, there we are. Everything we experience is for our awakening, an opportunity to see ourselves *again*. It's critical to wake up and get off this wheel of suffering. Until we do, we repeat every class in the School of Life over and over until we pass. Every class is ultimately about freedom.

Most of humanity seems lost in the rat race that no one wins. The wheel of suffering turns continuously, whether you are aware of it or not. Similar thoughts lead to similar actions with the same unsatisfactory results. Chained to the wheel of samsara, we experience rage, despair, and exhaustion over and over again. At some point, we reach the boiling point and it becomes a matter of life and death to stop. The good thing is that we can stop the wheel by paying attention to what we are doing. You have within you the power to make a new choice.

If we plant apple seeds, no matter how much we might want oranges, we'll get an apple tree and, eventually, apples. To grow oranges, we have to plant orange seeds. With wisdom, we understand which seeds produce which fruits. What are the consequences of our actions? If we want happiness and love, we need to plant wholesome seeds. When our actions are motivated by greed, hatred, or delusion, we are planting unwholesome seeds. It's not about good, bad, right, or wrong. Things unfold according to causes and conditions and they have consequences. Life is governed by these principles. We reap what we sow. Life unfolds in an organic fashion based on which seeds we plant. When we pay attention to the seeds, choosing and planting wisely, we can stop the wheel of samsara.

Once we calm our minds and see the seeds we are planting, we become master gardeners and naturally move toward healthier, more loving actions that cause us and others less pain. We don't do this because we *should,* but because we see clearly the consequences of our decisions and our actions. A truly wise person knows the difference between seeds that lead to happiness and seeds that lead to suffering and refrains from actions that lead to suffering. Developing wisdom takes time; feeling into what to do in each moment takes practice. We learn as we go.

The School of Life exists solely for our awakening; in truth there are no mistakes. When we tune into the flow that is carrying us along, we begin to notice everything in our lives helping us to wake up. We stop clinging to things we don't need, and suddenly the people and resources we do need may appear. The more we get out of the way, the more life flows toward and through us. And when things don't go well, we trust that too. We stop fighting against life and align ourselves with what's happening and trust that it's all for our healing and awakening. We begin to pay attention and to understand the lesson in every encounter.

Three things cannot be hidden for long; the sun, the moon, and the truth.

**—ANONYMOUS**

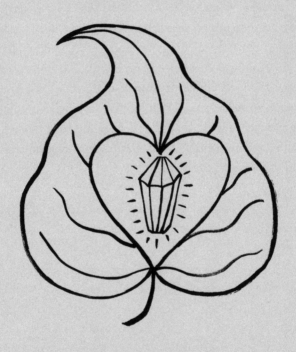

## CHAPTER FIVE

# REMEMBER WHO YOU ARE

A FRIEND SENT ME A PHOTO of a beautiful star twinkling in the night sky. "I found an old picture of you," she wrote. "Here you are a trillion years ago." When a star explodes at the end of its life, it scatters its elements throughout the universe, and that is what forms planets. We're literally made of stardust. It really was a picture of me, and of everyone.

On the opening night of my first meditation retreat, Jack Kornfield began his talk by quoting from a famous text: "O nobly born, remember who you are."[1] When I heard those words, something deep inside me was touched, unlocking memories of another time and place, if not another dimension. Somehow, I was reminded of my real self. Now, whenever I lead retreats, I tell people I'm simply reminding them of what they already know and who they truly are. The Buddha said we're all buddhas by nature, but we've forgotten. Unlock your memory and reconnect with your true self.

The root word *buddh* means "to wake up." It's a mind state, not a person; it's someone awake to their true self. You don't have to identify with any religion or even understand Buddhist teachings to appreciate this idea. There have been millions of awakened beings in the past and there will be millions more in the future. *Buddha nature* means that at the core of every human being is the clarity, radiance, compassion, and all-knowing wisdom that is our truest essence. We're really like that, but our radiance can be obscured. Meditation practice is to uncover the jewel in the heart of your lotus—to wake up.

Truth can never be destroyed, but it can be forgotten. It's crucial that we begin to wake up and remember. My soul friend and wise elder Alice Walker once said, "The main way people give up their power is by thinking they have none." It's easy to forget your light and your innate goodness, especially if you're a person of color, LGBTQ, or someone in a marginalized group. We get trapped in lies that we, and others, repeat—in the form of religious ideologies or in white supremacy, misogyny, and other forms of discrimination. I feel it is my sacred duty to remind you of your beauty, and I will do so until my last dying breath. Every human being of every ethnic background, gender, or sexual orientation, is at their fundamental core radiant, wise, and inherently buddha.

Many years ago, a good friend and I went on a spiritual pilgrimage to India. We were joined by other friends along the way. We visited Lumbini, where the Buddha was born; Varanasi, where he gave his first Dharma talk; Kushinagara, where he passed away; and Bodh Gaya, where he attained enlightenment. Bodh Gaya is in Bihar, the poorest state in India. The streets there are packed with beggars, hungry children, neglected animals, and piles of trash. Despite all that, it's one of the holiest pilgrimage sites in India, and it draws thousands and thousands of visitors every year from every corner of the world. At the center of Bodh Gaya there's a beautiful park with a garden, a huge, dome-shaped shrine called a *stupa*, and the great Bodhi tree, which is a descendant of the tree Siddhartha sat under when he attained enlightenment. Bodh Gaya is a deeply moving place to visit and it stands as a reminder, a symbol of our own infinite potential.

Around the Bodhi tree, there's a large grassy area where teachings, gatherings, and ceremonies are held. At any given time, hundreds of people are doing full prostrations as they face the tree. When you do full prostrations in the Tibetan style, it's like a yoga sun salutation. You place your palms together, fingers pointing upward, and then touch your hands to your forehead (your third eye), your heart, and finally you stretch out on the ground facedown. Bowing is a practice of surrendering your ego every time your forehead and your heart touch the earth. My friends and I spent hours there every day, meditating, talking, and reflecting on the life of the Buddha. On our third day, an impulse arose in me to offer 1,008 prostrations, 1,008 being an auspicious number in Asian traditions, and my friends encouraged me to do it. So, the next morning I began.

I arrived as soon as the park opened and found a nice spot with an available prostration board, and next to me was a smiley Tibetan woman who must have been ninety-years old. Not long after I began, hundreds of monks and nuns began prostrating alongside me, all of us facing the great Bodhi tree and bobbing up and down with full ceremonial exertion. Small pictures of the Buddha were placed everywhere, and a radiant-looking man in brown robes was purifying our prayers with a huge incensor while chanting *Om Mani Padme Hum*, Homage to the Jewel in the Lotus. Clouds of sweet-smelling smoke billowed in every direction. On the far side of the park, another group of monks were chanting the mantra that completes the Heart of Wisdom Sutra. *Gate Gate Paragate Parasamgate Bodhi Svaha*, "Gone, Gone, Gone Beyond,

Gone Altogether Beyond, O What an Awakening, Hail!" It is one of my favorite prayers, representing the perfection of wisdom, wisdom beyond wisdom.

After about fifty deep prostrations, I began to feel muscle strain, but I had committed to offering 1,008 bows, so I soldiered on. Every time I did another fifty, I'd stop for a breath and then continue. The devotional energy in the air was palpable. It was a religious marathon, all these people prostrating hour after hour. From time to time, some sweet person would come by with a gigantic tray offering everyone chai, and most of us would take a break to enjoy a cup of delicious, spicy Indian milk tea.

I went back to bowing, and after a while began to wonder, "What am I bowing to? Why am I doing this? Why am I even here?" I'd stop bowing, reflect for a moment, and say to myself things like, "I'm bowing to end suffering." I kept having inner conversations like this and responding. "Freedom," "Refuge," and on and on. It was getting increasingly challenging physically, but a kind of power was building inside me, and tears began to flow.

The heat of the day was intense, but I wasn't stopping and no one else was either. Through the sweat and the tears, I continued to ask, "What am I bowing to?" and respond, "Faith in something bigger than anything I've known before." Thoughts of being black, unwanted, and a woman all began to rise. "That's a big story," I told myself, "but there's a much bigger story," and I continued to feel the power of prayer and stayed with it. I prostrated for hours—even the next day, when I got up and went to the Bodhi tree again, I was still in a deep, reflective state: "Who am I? What am I bowing to?"

My friends were circumambulating the stupa and could see me bowing in the sea of people. I was in this profound state of absorption, looking up at the tree, tired, but continuing to prostrate, when I heard a familiar voice shout out, "Go Springers!" I looked up and saw my friends cheering me on, and I was like, "Right. Thanks guys."

I was in the deepest moment of my life, and they were shouting, "You can do it!" Even that became part of my inquiry, and it made me cry. As I kept prostrating, it finally dawned on me, "I am bowing to something that can never be destroyed." I too have within me the potential to be free. In that moment, I saw the jewel in the heart of the lotus, and it was my own goodness, my own compassionate heart. No one can take that light from me because it's indestructible.

In that moment, I realized that we all have a great power inside of us. We each carry immeasurable reserves of wisdom and courage. We have our share of suffering, but we are more than that. We are more than our stories, more than our traumas, more than our suffering. The seed that the Buddha uncovered is within you, within me, and within every living being. It is the seed of innate truth and it only needs to be nourished and watered. We are the sons and daughters of the universe. I bowed so much that day I thought my arms would fall off, but I kept going, bowing to the power that is within all beings.

We must *remember* who we really are. We are not just the story we've lived so far; our life is an epic tale with many chapters—many lifetimes—and we are here on the brink of time. To remember who we are is to reclaim our power, our truth, and our heart! César Chávez framed it this way, "Once change begins, it cannot be reversed. You cannot un-educate the person who has learned to read. You cannot humiliate the person who feels pride. You cannot oppress the people who are not afraid anymore."[2]

If we lose touch with our innate beauty and no longer see the truth of who we are, we must remember to look deeply within until the jewel in the lotus reveals itself again. It's difficult not to get carried away by the stream of media, politics, friends, and family. Meditation practice doesn't change anything around us. It simply reminds us who we already are—and *that* can change everything. The Buddha describes his teachings as a path of awakening that got covered over with leaves and debris. If we don't walk on the path and clear it once in a while, the way will be forgotten. Like any forest path, it has to be maintained and the signposts have to be reestablished. The Buddha didn't invent the path. He discovered what he and others had forgotten. This truth is ancient, perhaps older than the universe. Faith reminds us to believe in something bigger than our story line.

There was a golden statue of the Buddha cast in Siam (now Thailand) in the fourteenth century and installed in a temple in Ayutthaya, one hundred miles north of Bangkok. In the eighteenth century, the Ayutthaya Kingdom was invaded by Burma, so the statue was plastered over and painted to prevent it from being stolen. The temple remained in ruins for almost two hundred years and the statue was forgotten. In 1955, as it was about to be moved to a new location and the statue was being taken from its pedestal, the ropes broke, and it fell to the ground. At that moment, some of the plaster chipped off, allowing the gold Buddha underneath to be seen. The plaster was carefully removed, and when the statue was restored, its power and dignity became a source of inspiration for the local community and for people from all over the world.

About ten years ago, I was on a six-month retreat at the Forest Refuge, a small center in the woods in Massachusetts that's part of the Insight Meditation Society. I'd been sitting with a number of Burmese monks and was having a crisis of faith. "I can't do this anymore," I thought. I felt I had nothing left and wanted to get out of there. I didn't want to be with my mind anymore and I lost faith in myself and the path. I had worked myself into a frenzy and was having a complete meltdown.

We're typically discouraged from reading on retreats, but I went into the center's library to check out the small collection of serious Buddhist books. I so craved words that I had been reading signs like, "Don't put your shoes here," and even the ingredients on shampoo bottles. I was looking for *anything* to distract myself.

Walking among the library's bookshelves, I spotted a little book almost hidden between two larger books, titled *The Camel Knows the Way*. I thought, "I'm going to read this!" I ran back to my room, book in hand, and dove into this magical story.[3]

It was a beautiful book about a woman and her twenty-five-year friendship with Mother Teresa. The author, an Englishwoman, was a philanthropist who would attend Buddhist retreats and then fly to Calcutta to work with Mother Teresa and her Missionaries of Charity. She'd volunteer at the orphanages, help the sisters pick up people from the streets, and then in the evenings, she and Mother Teresa would have tea and talk about compassion. She wanted to have the Buddha's heart of compassion and the Christ consciousness of love and service, and was trying to integrate these paths. After a few months in Calcutta, she'd feel overwhelmed by all the suffering and would run off, exactly the way I was feeling. During one of these times, she arranged to do a pilgrimage across the desert, as the Desert Fathers had done centuries ago.

She hired a guide and his son to accompany her, and the plan was that they would caravan through the desert on camels. Her guides spoke almost no English, just a few simple words, so they mostly just gestured and smiled at each other. They'd get up each morning as the sun rose, have tea and breakfast, and then ride on their camels. At sundown, they would stay at various places or make camp, and she would read and write in her journal while the father and son would build a fire and talk. Things went well for the first seven days.

On the eighth morning, the guides helped her onto her camel, smacked the animal on the butt, and the camel began walking. Then the guides took off in the opposite direction, and she became alarmed. "Where are you going?" she asked, and the father answered in English, "The camel knows the way." "Oh, my God," she cried out. "You can't just leave me!" But they did.

For the next fifteen hours, she felt rage, then despair. "I'm going to die out here." She saw no one and did not have faith the camel knew the way. She began crying and feelings of fear overwhelmed her. She couldn't get off; she didn't know if bandits would come and kill her. All these emotions and thoughts, one after another, were flooding her.

She had a small canteen filled with water and a little snack pack, so she wasn't starving, and after hours of rage and panic, she started to think of the teachings of Mother Teresa. "If I'm going to die out here, is this the way I want to die? I want to live the teachings I've received, to benefit from all the work I've done." She started to reflect on the conversations they'd had. Mother Teresa was always telling her, "Have faith, open your heart, trust," and so she started to do just that. Mother Teresa always told her she had a beautiful heart, not only full of love but also wisdom. Until that moment, she hadn't believed her.

Over the next few hours, her heart had a profound awakening. She thought of the teachings of the Buddha and all the great masters she'd met, of Jesus and Mary, and the magic of the life she'd been given, and a deep gratitude began to arise. She felt thankful for all the gifts, and in her mind she was preparing to die. She was certain the camel would wander forever until she was dehydrated, and she was preparing herself for that. "If I'm going to die, I'll die with memories of the beauty I've had in my life, these wonderful teachings and this path. I'll die with prayers of love and devotion on my lips. I'm not going to go out a screaming, hysterical mess." By the time the sun began to set slowly and the sky was beginning to darken, she had completely let go. She was praying, holding Mother Teresa in her hand and the Buddha in her heart. She felt exhausted, when suddenly she saw the twinkling of lights in the distance. The camel continued walking, bringing her to the exact village, at the time designated on her itinerary. The camel indeed knew the way.

◯◯◯

I had started to lose faith, to question everything, to feel the suffering, and I wondered, "What's it all for?" I was lost and I'd forgotten my heart. The book about the camel reminded me of my path again and I rededicated myself to opening my heart. Our heart longs to be free. When it can't be free, it gets sick. We have to bow to the deepest potential in ourselves, to find those layers and open to the truth and beauty of them. Buddha nature is not only in us but in every other living being as well. Faith is like a giant candle, with a wick that lights a thousand other lights, spreading out infinitely.

What camel in your life knows the way? Climb onto it and ride it home, into your deepest self. Unlock your ancient memories and remember your true purpose. It's time to reclaim our place in this world. *O nobly born, remember who you are.* We are stardust. We are the sons and daughters of the Awakened Ones. Remember your heart of gold.

To go into the dark with a light is to know the light.
To know the dark, go dark. Go without sight,
and find that the dark, too, blooms and sings,
and is traveled by dark feet and dark wings.

—WENDELL BERRY

CHAPTER SIX

# INTO THE UNDERWORLD

MY FIRST NIGHT IN THE AMAZON rainforest was a mix of fear, excitement, and awe. I was attempting to sleep in my tiny wooden hut, huddled under a mosquito net and lying on a lumpy, damp mattress. With no electricity, I was engulfed in darkness, and the sounds of the forest around me were indescribable, otherworldly sounds—monkeys, frogs, insects, and God knows what. In spite of being completely exhausted from the long flight, the boat ride, and the hike into our jungle camp, I knew sleep would never come. The heat and humidity were suffocating, something was chewing on my roof, and a strange looking insect kept biting my ankles. I was in a different world and didn't know whether to laugh or burst into tears. I seriously started to question my sanity. What in the hell was I doing here?

My journey to the rainforest had begun after an intense, three-month meditation in Massachusetts the year before. It was during that particular time that I came face to face with a lot of not-yet-processed trauma. I was already a Dharma teacher and had spent a decade practicing meditation, and I thought I had already transformed this suffering. But the terror, grief, and abandonment I felt were so debilitating, I knew I needed something more, a different approach. I realized that some childhood wounds are so deep and traumatic that a special kind of intervention is needed. I didn't know what was happening any more, and I returned to California in a state of dread and panic. I don't know why I was so drawn to shamanism, but my intuition kept telling me I'd find answers there. So I decided to seek out the guidance of a shaman or a medicine woman to help me understand what was happening to me. Shortly after returning home from my retreat, a dear friend, a psychologist, told me she'd done some powerful healing work in Peru. A few months later, I was on a plane to the Amazon rainforest.

Over and over in indigenous stories, folklore, and world mythology, we encounter legends of the underworld—desolate places hidden deep in the earth that represent darkness, sometimes called the "Kingdom of the Dead." For unfortunate souls lost or trapped there, it's a terrible nightmare that never ends, a place with no hope of escape, no light, joy, or happiness. After an eternity of sorrow, the dead slowly dissolve into dust. In various legends, the underworld is watched over by a powerful god or guardian. In Greek mythology, it's Hades, whose primary function is to increase the number of souls in his kingdom and to be sure no one ever leaves.

From a psychological point of view, the underworld represents everything we don't see, acknowledge, or understand within ourselves. It's everything in our mind that is hidden, everything that's hiding in the shadows. Using shamanic language, we'd say that everything we are unaware of is *dark* and all we are aware of is *light*. The underworld is the doorway between the conscious and the unconscious dimensions of the mind-made worlds in which we live. Our deepest pain and core traumas lie in the underworld of our body, mind, and spirit.

I see the mind as a gigantic filing cabinet with an elaborate system of organization. We have access to certain files, the ones we use every day, which present no stress or problems. These files are stored near the front of the cabinet and are easy to locate when needed. We can call these our "conscious" files. We depend heavily on our conscious files, and they help us navigate life and make sense of things.

A larger number of files are stored near the back of the cabinet, hidden from view, and usually inaccessible to us. These are the "unconscious" files. We also use these every day, but without awareness. They have a life of their own. There are two kinds of unconscious files. Some contain truth, love, and beauty and others contain pain, darkness, and trauma. A goal of the spiritual path, the journey to wholeness, is to uncover, reveal, and integrate all the files in our cabinet, especially the unconscious files, both positive and negative.

Some unconscious files may contain light that is more beautiful that we can stand. Visions of angelic beings or experiences of love, heaven, or oneness can sometimes create fear or doubt, so they get buried as well. All the parts of ourselves that we are unable to handle are buried there. We want to be loved, accepted, and approved of, so the mind creates this elaborate filing system to help us fit in. Over time, we might bury so much of ourselves that we become depressed, disconnected, and confused, leading to the overwhelming feeling of being lost. Eventually we might shut down completely.

On a regular basis, in an attempt to help us function in the world, our mind buries information in the unconscious files. Many of the difficult childhood experiences and events that traumatized us are buried there. The word *trauma* describes experiences so emotionally distressing that they exceed our ability to cope. These are events that are outside of "normal" human experiences. Physical and sexual abuse, rape, violence, assaults, near-death experiences, accidents, war, and medical procedures can create deep traumas. As children, we are particularly vulnerable to these experiences and unless the emotions are resolved, they can impact the rest of our life. Painful experiences of our ancestors are also in our unconscious files, hidden from view.

Whole communities or ethnic groups can also participate in burying things in unconscious files. Injustice, discrimination, and the politics of war are often denied and buried in the collective unconscious. Corporations that destroy the planet and then hide the evidence are also burying things in the collective unconscious files. Humankind is suffering from collective heartbreak; years of so many buried memories, destroyed dreams, and a lack of compassion have taken their toll. A society that participates in war, in the destruction of its own environment, a collective filled with sexism, homophobia, racism, and classism is symptomatic of our collective heartbreak. Individual and collective trauma shuts down our ability to give and receive love.

The part of ourselves most likely to get lost in the underworld is our heart. I saw this clearly while working with the shamans I met during my first trip to the jungle. My heart was so wounded, I knew the only way to rescue it was to feel everything that was keeping it closed. At some point, we all have to embark upon the heroic journey to regain all we have lost. To heal, we need to descend into the land of the dead and recover the buried and fragmented pieces of our hearts. No matter how hard you try to bury things, it all eventually surfaces. And besides, we're always *feeling* what is happening on an energetic level, whether we are aware of it are not.

The doorways between worlds are always open. In shamanic cultures and mythology, we are summoned to the underworld for specific reasons. Once we decide to pursue understanding and freedom, we can no longer run from ourselves and the battle lines are drawn. We go into the underworld to make a daring rescue—to reclaim our courage and our power. We travel there to rescue the parts of ourselves that we have forgotten or neglected and which are now in jeopardy, slowly dying.

In the Shipibo communities of the Upper Amazon region of Peru, shamans travel to the underworld during sacred ceremonies on behalf of the sick. In a heightened state, the shaman is able to locate and retrieve the spirit of the patient. This is called a "soul retrieval," and I have experienced this type of healing directly. After participating in this sacred ceremony, the patient begins to recover from the physical or mental suffering she was experiencing.

We go to the underworld to become free. We walk through the swamps and encounter the forces that operate within us. It's the way we heal ourselves, the path of purification. We don't get to choose what will be purified: "Please put my mother issues in a nice container, and I'll take it to go, but leave the divorce (or whatever is the most difficult) for later." In meditation, we see the most painful *and* blissful aspects of our life in high def 3-D through repetitive thoughts, stories, and emotions. We feel the pain from our families and communities, the ethnic groups we belong to, the pain of the Earth pulsating in our bones. When our body begins to open, we feel it through all the sensations we've been unable to access until now. We enter the underworld through our body and through our mind, opening doors and windows that have been locked for years, if not centuries. It's scary but it's exciting at the same time.

At some point, we enter the epicenter of our mind, the eye of the hurricane. Habitual ways of thinking, addictions, and the other ways we fall into darkness can help lead us to find the root, but we can't just *look* down at it. We need to discover the source of our suffering and *uproot* it. For thousands of years, shamans have facilitated death-and-rebirth experiences. At each stage of our life's journey, aspects of ourselves, including core beliefs, negative habits, dysfunctional relationships, and even the person we thought we were—what we think of as our identity, "us," "me" "myself"—needs to die so that new life can come forth.

The Gnostic Gospels say, "If you bring forth that which is within you, then that which is within you will be your salvation. If you do not bring forth that which is within you, then that which is within you will destroy you."[1] We need to find the courage and compassion to look at the forces that operate with impunity within us. It's the way to heal ourselves.

On a retreat I led a few years ago, I met a courageous woman named Kafira. She was born in Israel and had been living in Brooklyn for years. She was tall and athletic with that distinct New York edge that comes from years of urban living. She had become extremely depressed and described to me how she'd begun to mutilate herself. She would pull her hair and hurt her body in ways that frightened her. During our conversations, she shared that at the age of eighteen, she was drafted into the Israel Defense Forces special operations unit. The violence she participated in and the horrors she witnessed during her deployment were unbelievable. When her service ended, she left Israel, cut all ties to her homeland, and never looked back. She had blocked everything out in an attempt to move on, but the trauma she carried for so long was resurfacing. During the retreat, she realized how much her military experience had affected her whole life. She was unable to have intimate relationships, was frequently angry, and had lost faith in humankind. Worst of all, she hated herself for what she had done as a soldier.

I encouraged her to practice self-compassion and allow herself to be present for the memories she had blocked out for so long. As the fear, anger, and grief began to arise, she started to open to it instead of fight it. She began to feel again and was able to grieve compassionately for the eighteen-year-old girl who had endured so much. She discovered that going into the pain was healing and, with each courageous step she took, her beautiful heart began to open more and more.

Jack Kornfield says, "We must shed the past over and over again."[2] Doing so moves us to a higher state of consciousness, and with it comes more understanding of who we really are. What follows death is always rebirth, and that's what makes the cycle so powerful. The caterpillar morphs into the butterfly, and with faith and trust we can experience transformations like this ourselves. There is an intelligence that supports us as we move rhythmically from one stage of life to the next. The universe moves and dances, and we shift and dance to the same rhythm. Periods of expansion are followed by periods of contraction; nothing stays still for long. Everything moves in and out of cycles of death and rebirth.

Navigating our way through the shadows is where we reclaim our own light. It's in the shadows and the darkness that we learn who we truly are. All our experiences have value. The most painful ones are grist for the mill, sacred compost. Our suffering, past and present, allows us to open, and thus to grow. It's all part of the healing process. In Twelve Step recovery programs there is a saying that you're only as sick as your secrets. I believe this to be true.

It's time to let go of everything that is holding us back. We can no longer run from ourselves; Pandora's box has been opened and now we all have to dance in the dark. We're all in the underworld now, so trust that your fierce heart will lead the way.

The Buddha said that the past is already gone, the future is not yet here; there is only one moment for you to live: that is the present moment.

—THICH NHAT HANH

CHAPTER SEVEN

# THE TIME IS NOW

A FRIEND ONCE SENT ME A CARTOON that shows three booths at a spiritual fair. The sign at the first booth says "Past-Life Readings," and there's a long line waiting to get in. The second says "Future-Life Readings," and it too has a long line. The third booth reads "Present Moment," and there's no one there. To live in the present moment requires courage, practice, and dedication. Much of the time, our crazy monkey mind is chatting about past and future, past and future, past and future. *What have I done? What's going to happen?* The Buddha's radical response, whether we're bored, brokenhearted, angry, frustrated, or lonely, is to be here now.

When I began to practice meditation, I had no idea what I was doing. I'd sit down and think about all my problems, endlessly reliving past dramas and anticipating future great adventures. I did this over and over for hours at a time, and once in a while for a few amazing minutes, my mind would become quiet and I'd feel a profound happiness. In spite of not knowing what I was doing, I hung in there, just to experience those moments of happiness, moments when I was truly present. It wasn't until I met my first teachers that I began to understand that thinking is not the point of meditation.

Lady Luck was on my side. In my early twenties, I met two wonderful meditation teachers, Jack Kornfield and Joseph Goldstein. Jack is a psychologist, Buddhist scholar, and meditation genius. Over the years, he has been a father figure for me and guided me along the path of becoming a meditation teacher. His years of training and his ongoing support have been invaluable. He is a true gift to me and to the world. Joseph Goldstein is one of the great Western teachers, having himself studied for decades with masters from India, Burma, and Tibet. He was the one person who helped me with my meditation practice on long retreats. Joseph and Jack have been friends with each other since the sixties, when along with two other teachers, they founded the Insight Meditation Society (IMS), a large center in Barre, Massachusetts. IMS offers retreats year-round, and every fall they have a three-month-long silent, intensive meditation course. Joseph has guided me during all of my long retreats and taught me the nuts and bolts of meditation.

After my first meditation retreat in the desert, I knew I wanted more. I was strongly motivated to heal from my pain through understanding the Buddha's teachings and practices. In the fall of 1999, I signed up for my first three-month retreat at IMS. I was a little freaked out about being in silence for three months, but somewhere deep inside I knew I could do it and that my heart wanted it more than anything.

I arrived in the tiny town of Barre and discovered that I was the youngest person at the retreat by thirty-five years and the only person of color. I felt so out of place I began to doubt the whole thing—the people, the teachers, the program. I'd left my colorful community in Oakland behind, and I was filled with harsh judgments about these old people wearing dingy clothes and walking around in slow motion. I was sure I'd made a huge mistake. Maybe I should have gone to India or the Himalayas, places with real gurus and way cooler people. I couldn't imagine how I would survive this place for a week, let alone three months.

The schedule was intense. We woke up at 5:00 a.m. and went to bed at 10:00 p.m. There was an hour of sitting meditation, followed by an hour of very slow walking meditation, and just that, on and on, all day long. We had breaks for meals but we were supposed to practice eating meditation during that time. Every evening, one of the teachers would give an hour-long Dharma talk to share aspects of meditation and core Dharma teachings.

On the first night, I got to see Joseph Goldstein and listen to him teach. I'm not sure what I was expecting; I had only seen a black-and-white headshot of him in a newsletter. But I was caught off guard by how regular he and all the other teachers were, not at all like my idea of Indian gurus. He didn't have flowing, long hair and wasn't wearing holy-looking robes, prayer beads, or any spiritual garb at all. He looked so regular I couldn't believe it. He was dressed in khaki pants and a plaid shirt. He didn't even look hippieish or sound New Agey; he didn't use words like *energy, chakra,* or *vibration.* He had a deep baritone voice with an east coast accent that reminded me of one of my college professors. This was the great Joseph Goldstein? I had my doubts.

Despite these and so many other uncertainties, I had to admit Joseph had some serious meditation credentials. He had spent ten years studying in India with some of the greatest meditation masters of the twentieth century. He had authored some excellent meditation books and had been practicing for decades. In spite of my bad attitude, I recognized that he was all I had and I'd better listen to him. Someone was going to have to help me get through those next three months, and it might as well be him.

Over and over I coaxed myself: *Come back to the breath. You can do it. Sit. Walk. Sit.* It took a week before my mind went totally insane. I couldn't understand what the teachers were saying; they kept obsessing about the present moment. *What has that got to do with anything?* The few times I was present, I felt an agonizing throb in my hip, volcanic anger, and a sharp stabbing in my heart. It was not fun.

My mind simply wouldn't stop thinking. It kept exploding into thoughts, one after another—and they were manic, moving at five hundred miles an hour. I saw parts of movies, heard music sound bytes, and relived memories of the fourth grade, a trip to Mexico, ice cream sundaes, on and on endlessly. Thousands and thousands of thoughts burst forth like an insane kaleidoscope. It was painful and, most of all, exhausting. My head pounded and my stomach was in knots. All I wanted to do was go home, lie on my couch, watch TV, and eat chocolate. I was genuinely confused. *Why am I putting myself through this?*

By the time I had my first meeting with Joseph, I was a wreck, completely humbled and desperate for advice. During that meeting, all my doubts about him were destroyed. He was wise, kind, and extremely patient with me. After I described my hellish experiences over the previous days, he just smiled. His advice was simple. "Instead of reacting to everything that is happening in the mind, try to become mindful," become aware and accepting of whatever is happening in the present moment. He encouraged me to notice each emotion and body sensation, regardless of whether it was pleasant or unpleasant.

When we feel angry, we often act out. We're on a roller coaster ride, reacting to everything that appears in the mind. We direct our rage at others, verbally and sometimes physically, or we try to bury it deep down. When someone who's repressing anger has a smile on their face, you can feel the rage seething beneath the surface, it carries a strong energy.

Mindfulness meditation offers a third way to respond to emotions. Instead of reacting or suppressing our emotions, we open to them. We learn to *feel* our anger, allowing it to be there for as long as it wants. This is a challenge. When we feel something painful, we want to get rid of it. Meditation teaches us to open as a witness and, if we start to react, to observe that. If we get angry, we notice that anger is present. That's all. We greet every experience with respect, working skillfully with whatever is arising. Someone acts in a way we don't like and we feel a strong sensation of anger: our hearts beat, our breathing gets fast, and we feel like reacting strongly right away. With mindfulness, we become aware of our emotions and learn to wait until the feeling dissipates, so that we can engage more skillfully with the other person.

*Vipassana* is a Pali word that means "clear seeing," being with life as it is. We're training our minds to be open, to be with what's happening right now. Meditation teaches us how to be present. Using the body and the breath as objects, we cultivate awareness. Throughout the day we have the tendency to brace ourselves, and this tension is our armor. In meditation, we ease ourselves into comfort. We learn how to be.

People often come to retreats with an agenda—healing difficult relationships, overcoming health issues, desiring mystical states. Sometimes we "meditate" to escape or experience blissful sensations; we want to enter the light or transport ourselves to another time and space. We don't want to feel the pain of our lives, so we try to meditate to numb ourselves. But meditation practice is not an escape; it's the opposite. True practice is learning to turn towards whatever is rising in the moment. It's learning to be with the truth of things. This path is about meeting your life, feeling what's happening in the present moment. As you sit, emotions, often taking the form of bodily sensations, will arise. Be open to them. Be with what is. Stay present, whether you feel agitated, excited, or bored.

Be with the boredom; hold it with love and nonviolence. Open to each moment even when it's difficult. It can even be difficult to open to love and happiness. Whatever arises, allow and be present with it. Meditation is a pathway to inner peace, but it takes patience and practice.

Imagine a palace ten stories high with thousands of rooms. And imagine that for your whole life, you've lived in a single, tiny basement room and have never gone upstairs. In fact, you didn't even know there was an upstairs. Then one day, you feel an impulse to look around, and you discover this vast, unlived-in space. You've done your best to keep things in your little room tidy, but as you climb up to the rest of the house, you see that it's in terrible shape. The rooms have been abandoned for so long, there are massive amounts of dust, creepy crawlers, and just plain junk. Roaming the different levels, you're shocked by the volume of trash, and at the same time exhilarated to see the potential. You get out your broom, dust rags, and mop and get to work.

The thousand-room palace is our mind, and this massive spring-cleaning is part of meditation, the "path of purification." We explore all that has accumulated and decide what to keep and what to let go of. We discard layers of debris, some inherited from our ancestors; some from our childhood, some societal, and some residue from the state of our world. Regardless of how each piece of junk got there or to whom it belongs, it is our sacred task to clean it all up.

As we move from room to room, we face painful memories, some of which we've never shared with anyone else. After all these years, we feel our feelings, and it can trigger tears, terror, or rage. It isn't easy to allow such strong emotions to move through us, but this is part of the healing process. Everything that has ever affected us physically or emotionally can be experienced as compressed energy being released. Allowing and accepting it all is vital. As each layer comes into awareness, sensations, memories, emotions, energy, and at times altered states of consciousness might arise. The mind goes through its shedding process. Sometimes the body follows; sometimes it leads. Layers of fear, rage, sorrow, and hopelessness can arise, and with the steadiness of mind developed through practice, we are able to allow this purification process to take place.

There is beauty and honesty in this journey. We shed the masks we've worn—masks of ignorance, confusion, and other layers that obscure the truth. We take down our smoke screens, our habitual defenses, so that we can no longer hide from the things in our own minds. Our ways of deceiving ourselves, and others, dissipate, and we feel entirely vulnerable. There is a nakedness in encountering the truth of the moment. Sad memories still come up for me as well as the pain of my mother, my father, my grandfather. But it doesn't hurt as much as before because I've learned to bear witness, to sit like a buddha and ride out the storms. Meditation reminds me to listen, to wake up and pay attention, to remember that I'm part of the human family, connected to all of creation with its beauty and tragedy, suffering and freedom.

> To begin, just sit comfortably on a chair or a cushion. It helps if your back is aligned; this allows the energy in the body to move freely. Close your eyes lightly, take a deep breath in and a deep breath out, and with your mind's eye, feel the breathing and the sensations in your body. Relax your neck and shoulders; maybe move your neck a bit and gently rotate your shoulders. Relax your face and your jaw, your arms and your hands, letting the blood flow as you inhale and exhale. Settling this way calms your nervous system. Now relax your belly and bring your awareness there. We often tense these muscles, holding energy in our midsection. Releasing any

part of the body that's holding back energy can have a profound effect on our state of mind and our health. Let yourself arrive here from the busyness of the day. Bring your awareness inside you. Notice the rhythm of your breathing. Don't force it; this is not a breath exercise. Let your breathing be natural, relaxed. Just use the sounds you hear and the sensations you feel to help you be present. Observe the rising and falling of your abdomen with each breath. There's nowhere to go; just "be here now." Each time you notice your mind wandering, bring the focus gently back to a sensation, a feeling, or to your breathing. In mindfulness meditation, we return again and again to the breath, sensations, and sounds. As you breathe in, open to life as it is. It can be helpful to meditate for a set period of time, like twenty minutes or half an hour. Be gentle, have lightness of heart, and be kind toward your hard working body and mind. Be patient with yourself. Cultivating the mind is like tending a garden. At first, the soil is compacted and strewn with litter. The first stage is to sit and watch, to observe the garden of your mind. In doing so, you see that the mind has a mind of its own. You might think, "My mind is restless and crazy." That's okay. Open to that. It's organic and perfect. The next stage is to till the soil. Open to *whatever* is happening, whatever is present for you. Maybe you have a heavy heart, sadness, fear, or stress. You can learn to work with all these states; you don't need to repress them or try to escape. The way to freedom is always *through*, staying open to things as they are. We use our body as the ground to cultivate awareness. Our mind might be off somewhere else, but our body is always in the present moment.

Notice the rhythm of your breathing. You're not con-
trolling the breath. You're just becoming aware of it.
Notice where you feel the breath. It might be in your nose
or mouth, your chest or midsection. Sense the breath
rising and falling. There's no need to force or control
anything; each process has its own rhythm. As you sit,
sounds, sensations, thoughts, stories, and worries will
arise. Let them be in the background. When you find
that you're caught in a story or a sensation, return to your
breathing. Whatever happens—birds singing, even the
sounds of traffic or people talking—open to the present
moment. Meditation is not a task. We're not trying to
gain anything; we're just learning how to be present.

Sometimes while we're meditating, we doze off. We sit down, and
every now and then we get a moment that's clear, but once we get
quiet, it's, "Goodnight!" We're so stimulated so much of the time
that when we're in a warm, safe place, we breathe in and out and fall
asleep! The mind just shuts off. We have to work with a sleepy mind.
In our meditation practice, there are two energies which commonly
come up that we can learn to balance. One is sinking mind or sleepiness. The other is restlessness. We can't sit still. We want to run
out and scream, and we don't know why. Either of these two energies can make meditation difficult. Feel your body, breathe, open to
what is happening, and name it: "sleepiness" or "restlessness." These
are energies; we can get interested in them and in doing so, we wake
up the mind.

Find a time for practicing meditation that works for you. If
you're a morning person, meditate early. Some people sit as early as
5:00 a.m. If you're a night person, you might want to meditate
before going to bed. Find your rhythm, and meditate when your
mind is most clear. Start to practice for small amounts of time; five

or ten minutes a couple of times a day can be really powerful. Be gentle and kind in your awareness, friendly to your mind.

When we begin to live in the present moment, something transformative happens. We become more available to the wisdom and compassion that's within us. There is a shift in consciousness, an awareness of truth, and we see things differently. Even when we revert to the old patterns, we can return to the present and, instead of reacting, become mindful. When one big story or obsessive thought-train ends, and just before we get lost in the next one, there is a moment called now. Sometimes we tap into it effortlessly and at other times we do so through practicing meditation. The present moment is medicine for the mind. It purifies ignorance and we are able to see things as they are, not as we wish they were, or even as they might appear. We take in this medicine of the truth by dwelling deeply in the present moment, and it heals us. It's so simple we might overlook it. One breath, two breaths; one step, two steps, and the whole of the Dharma unfolds.

The devil whispers, you can't withstand the storm.
The warrior replies, I am the storm.

—ANONYMOUS

## CHAPTER EIGHT

# THE WHITE CONDOR

IN SHAMANIC CULTURES, an initiation is a rite of passage, a test, a stepping-stone, or a threshold that each of us must cross in life. An initiation often comes with challenges that bring us face-to-face with our worst fears. These transformative rites can include life-threatening experiences, and each initiate has to enter into the "dance of no hope" alone. It's called the dance of no hope because once it starts, it's no longer in our control and we are forced to surrender everything to a power unknown and bigger than ourselves. Standing at the crossroads with our will to live and our courageous heart is when we awaken the warrior within.

We embark upon this journey only after losing our guideposts, our bearings, when all we hold precious starts to fall away. For many, it comes suddenly, with no warning; our boat simply begins to sink. It can be triggered by relationships ending, financial collapse, a frightening diagnosis, violence, losing our home, acknowledgment of addiction, or a near-death experience. It forces us to question the very foundation of who we are.

We are being profoundly tested, and the further we journey, the less recognizable we are to others and the more recognizable we are to ourselves. Our buried giant is coming alive. If we are fortunate, resistance becomes less and less of an option. The only response is to open to the experience life has brought us, no matter how painful or desperate it appears to be. The darkest hour is the one before dawn. All initiations, no matter how sorrowful and dangerous, have a clear purpose, and that is to wake us up.

Once I decided to do a self-retreat for no other reason than that my life was falling apart and nothing else made sense. It all began when the man I loved flew across the world to tell me that he had fallen in love with another woman. He spent the next hour holding my hands and explaining why he thought it was best to move on with his life. Her name was Tami, a gorgeous yoga teacher who was many years younger than I. This was the man I thought was my soul mate and he was the only man that I have ever wanted to marry. To say I was madly in love was an understatement. At that moment in time he meant everything to me. I'd had plenty of break ups over the years but this was on a whole other level. The grief was primal; it hit me fast and hard. I collapsed on the ground, crying and clutching my heart.

I lay in bed for days sobbing, screaming into my pillow, and shaking uncontrollably. My heart was breaking, and the pain was unbearable. I was shattered. I couldn't eat or sleep, and thoughts of suicide came in waves. To make matters worse, I got into a car accident and began having debilitating pain in my stomach. A few days later at a doctor appointment, they discovered a growth in the lining of my uterus. It was very serious and I would need a hysterectomy. In a period of just three short weeks, everything around me came crashing down, and I entered into one of the darkest periods of my life.

I needed help. I decided to do a retreat up in the mountains in northern California because my crisis was becoming a matter of life and death. I took very little food for my week-long retreat. Fasting felt important, and I had no appetite anyway. I also took with me my medicine bag, my drum, eagle feathers, and Quan Yin statue. I planned on doing compassion practice and sitting in silence. I felt scared for myself because I was in such a dark place.

As the darkness of the first night approached, a hysterical laughter arose in me and with it screams of "Take me!!! Take me!" Over and over I shouted at God with a seething rage I had never experienced before. I could hear my screams echo all around me, and it just enraged me more. "Take me, motherfucker, take me!!!!" I screamed into the darkness until my voice gave out and my throat turned to sandpaper. Finally, exhausted, I wrapped my blanket around me and fell into a deep sleep.

Waking the next morning, I was sad and angry that I was still alive. God hadn't listened to me, and I cursed loudly. The sun was coming up and my body was sore, feverish, and weak. Eventually I sat up and noticed for the first time where I was. It was stunningly beautiful. I was in a tiny cottage under a large grove of redwood trees. They were huge old growth redwoods soaring high into the sky. There was a cliff nearby with spectacular views overlooking the wild forest below. There were majestic redwoods in all directions. It was untouched, primeval beauty. The sky was the most incredible shade of blue and there wasn't a cloud in sight. It was completely quiet except for the sounds of birds chirping in the distance. The beauty around me brought me waves of grief, and I spent most of the day huddled under my blanket weeping uncontrollably.

I wept for all the losses I had experienced throughout my life. I wept for the loss of my great love affair, the loss of my uterus, the loss of the children I would never have. I wept for the loss of my childhood. I spent the whole second day of my retreat weeping for everything I had ever lost. I just didn't understand how life could be so cruel. I tried so hard to be a good person and yet everything

I wanted so badly was gone. As night approached, I tried again to scream, but my voice was gone so I whispered over and over again, "Take me God; please be merciful and just take me; I don't want to be here anymore."

That night I had a dream, the first of a series of powerful dreams and visions. There was a white light that was so bright it was hard to look at. Within this light, I could see gigantic wings flapping very slowly. As I awoke the following morning, I was able to sit up for the first time in twenty-four hours. I felt lighter, and everything around me looked pristine and sharp.

During the night, my senses had magically become heightened. I could hear the sounds of the animals around me and feel the aliveness of everything. The land, the trees, the rocks, and even the sky all seemed alive. The air was so fresh that I kept taking deep breaths throughout the day. My body felt deprived of oxygen, and I gasped over and over to take in more and more air. A deep silence overtook me for most of the day, and my mind fell into a clear space with very few thoughts. It was a state similar to what I had experienced during a Vipassana meditation retreat I had done many years before.

Before I knew it, the sun began to set and again I curled up into my blanket and fell asleep. That night the dream appeared just as before. I could see this bright light and within it was the most beautiful bird I had ever seen. I recognized it as a condor from pictures I had seen in books. I'd only seen condors that were black, and this one was pure white. It was a female condor with a wingspan so wide it covered the entire sky. The beauty of this majestic creature overcame me as she began to reveal herself slowly, with more and more clarity. She smiled at me while hovering in the sky above, slowly flapping her enormous wings. The next morning when I awoke, the dream was fresh in my mind, and I felt the strong presence of this bird spirit throughout the day. I spent most of the day sitting on the deck staring off into the vast, blue sky. I felt neither hunger nor thirst, just a radical *presence* as my mind once again entered into a deep silence.

That night, as I wrapped myself in my blanket, I didn't pray for God to take me, just that I might meet the magical condor again. As I fell into a deep sleep, she appeared and this time with such vivid clarity that I knew she was real. She flew down and entered directly into my heart. The places in me that were shattered were penetrated by white light, and I realized she was healing my heart. I awoke the next morning with a smile and, for the first time in months, a sense of being happy to be alive.

After a few hours I took my seat in meditation, and she appeared again in the sky. I didn't know whether I was awake or dreaming, and at that point it didn't matter. She flew down into my heart again, and I shape-shifted into her. My head became hers, and I felt my face contort into a beak, my hands curled and became talons, and I felt my wings extend outward from my back. I didn't have time to be scared, because in one great leap I flew off the cliff and became this beautiful spirit soaring through the sky. I had heard of medicine men shape-shifting into jaguars and other animals, but I never thought I would experience something as sacred as this.

I spent the entire day soaring in the sky. I began to understand things I'd never known. How vast and profound this human life is. How vast the universe is. I understood that she was me, that this condor was my own spirit, and that I had to undergo all the challenges in order to set myself free. My heart had been shattered so that it could open, so that it could be put back together in a new way. The experiences that I had gone through were not meant to destroy me but to awaken me. I cried at the poignancy of this new understanding. I was shown many things that day about my future, what I had come here to do, and why everything happened the way it did. As the tears rolled down my cheeks, I knew for certain that everything would be okay.

Deep inside, we know that challenges can bring us closer to the truth that we are much stronger than we realize. It's only through being tested that we discover the unshakeable ground we stand on. We stand in the shoes of all the great beings who have come before, and now is our time to learn to stand tall and meet life with our own heart of courage. The Latin root of the word courage is *cor*, heart.

When we hit rock bottom, our heart opens. This is not a time to act spiritual; it's an opportunity to become fully honest and to compassionately review how you've lived your life. It can be painful, but it's an essential part of healing, of becoming whole, of including *all* of ourselves—all our experiences, all our traits, those we like and those we don't. Hitting bottom brings forth humility and surrender. We get down on our knees and with an open heart, we pray for help. This is life's mysterious way of pointing us in a new direction. We're on a sinking ship, afraid; but when we stop and genuinely ask for help, a rescue boat always appears. It's a painful but also a beautiful time when we openly surrender and ask for help. In that moment, we're choosing *life*.

Initiations are archetypal processes, and they appear in myths, fairytales, and stories throughout the world. But they are barely known of in the West today. Modern doctors and mental health practitioners often don't recognize them as life passages, cycles of growth and healing, but instead see them as symptoms of depression, mental breakdown, or midlife crisis. Instead of allowing this natural and necessary process to complete itself, they diagnose it, medicate it, shut it down, and stop or prolong what is already a painful experience.

When we are unable to see this initiation process all the way through, we can get energetically stuck. This dark night of the soul can take many forms—a life-threatening illness, an addiction, or an accident; it can be brought about by the death of a loved one, a break up, the loss of a home or a job, or by being in an abusive relationship. We hit rock bottom, everything comes crashing down, and we feel as though we're at the brink of life and death. This is a natural process, which benefits from the help of a spiritual intervention so we can let go of what needs to go and new parts of ourselves can be born. When we feel it's coming, if we choose to ignore it, we can become tortured, our mind might be in chaos, our emotions out of control, and we can get really angry. "Why is life doing this to me?" It feels like everything is against us, and we may want to give up.

During the process of an initiation, we might have visions of dying, suicidal thoughts, dreams of being killed, or in rare cases an actual near-death experience. We might display symptoms of depression, wanting to isolate ourselves, sleeping many hours a day, lying very still as though wrapped in a cocoon. Grief and despair can arise along with oceans of tears. We might be attracted to dead, unhealthy foods and temporarily lose energy and vitality. Life feels like it's spiraling downward, and no matter how hard we try to hold on, everything just keeps dissolving. It's important to understand that this is a temporary cycle and to have compassion, patience, and presence.

ꡀꡀꡀ

After making the painful decision to leave his royal palace, Prince Siddhartha stood on the riverbank, cut off his hair, and threw his royal clothing on the ground. He had reached a critical moment in his life's journey and it was time for him to let go of everything he had known until then—power, privilege, wealth, marriage, fatherhood, and his identity as the successor to his father's throne. Taking this step required enormous faith and courage, and it changed the course of history.

After Siddhartha let go of his life as a prince, he spent six long years in the forest practicing diligently and never wavering from his goal. His achievement under the Bodhi tree was astonishing. It is the ultimate death and rebirth story. Siddhartha vowed not to move until his heart was freed and he understood the true nature of reality. With the weapons of wisdom and compassion, Siddhartha battled the ferocious demon Mara into the night. Back and forth they went, Siddhartha was able to overcome all fear, lust, greed, hatred, and doubt, and as the sun began to rise in the east, a fully awakened being arose from under the Bodhi tree. The earth quaked in the four directions as another Buddha was born that day.

◯◯◯

As with all things, the painful times could not last forever. This dark period in my life gave birth to Lotus Vine Journeys, my Peru-based organization, in which I take students with me to explore the plant medicine world and wisdom of the Amazon region. In the midst of some of the worst moments in my life, this incredible vision of creating life-changing retreats focused on Buddhist wisdom and plant spirit medicine began to manifest. It was a dream I shared with the man I once loved so much but when he left it became my personal dream. Like the phoenix rising from the ashes, my dark night of the soul spawned one of the most creative periods in my life.

"Unconditional" by Jennifer Welwood

Willing to experience aloneness,
I discover connection everywhere;
Turning to face my fear,
I meet the warrior who lives within;
Opening to my loss,
I gain the embrace of the universe;
Surrendering into emptiness,
I find fullness without end.
Each condition I flee from pursues me,
Each condition I welcome transforms me
And becomes itself transformed
Into its radiant jewel-like essence.
I bow to the one who has made it so,
Who has crafted this Master Game;
To play it is purest delight;
To honor its form—true devotion.[1]

If you have come to help me, you are wasting your time. If you have come because your liberation is bound up with mine, let us work together.

—ABORIGINAL ACTIVIST GROUP, QUEENSLAND, 1975

## CHAPTER NINE

# MEETING THE GREAT CHIEF

"LOVE AND COMPASSION are necessities, not luxuries," says the Dalai Lama. "Without them humanity cannot survive."[1] Wise spiritual leaders radiate this precious quality, but so do millions of everyday people living simple lives with great heart. I refer to compassion as the Great Chief because with it we can become courageous in the face of overwhelming suffering. Once we truly encounter the Great Chief within ourselves, we can take the hand of others and help them. When we open to the depths of our own pain, we naturally become a refuge for others. We learn to open our heart to other people, because in truth we are all in this together.

My encounters with the Great Chief began at an early age. When I was thirteen, I fell madly in love with a fifteen-year-old boy. He ended up being my childhood sweetheart for many years. It was Valentine's Day, and I really wanted to give him a gift, but I had no money. So my best friend suggested I steal something for him. I had never shoplifted, but my friend's enthusiasm persuaded me to give it a try. Bad idea. I was caught immediately by the store security and taken to the police station, where my mother had to pick me up after she got off work. At this time my mother was a single parent working sixty hours a week, this was the last thing she needed to deal with. She was furious, and I remember her yelling angrily, "You're going to work this off, Spring!"

I agreed to do my fifty hours of community service at Glide Memorial Church, in the soup kitchen. Glide was, and still is, a beacon of hope and compassion in San Francisco's Tenderloin district. At the time, the Tenderloin was filled with drug addicts, prostitutes, and a lot of homeless people. Violence and despair were everywhere, and Glide dedicated itself to providing loving, compassionate outreach services to the community.

I showed up early on a Saturday morning ready to work off my debt to society. As I exited the car, my mother said, sternly, "You're going to mop, clean, and feed people." And I said, "All right, I'll do it." Actually, I was raring to go. It all seemed exciting for some reason, and in spite of it only being 8:00 a.m. in the morning, the Tenderloin was in full swing. There were dealers, hustlers, and people begging for money everywhere.

I went into the kitchen and met the other volunteer staff; and they smiled at me kindly. Many had scars and missing teeth; they'd all been through the depths of hell—former junkies and homeless people who were grateful to have found their way to Glide. They felt blessed to be clean, sober, and still alive. They all had so much joy! One man spoke about how in his worst moment, Jesus came down, kissed his cheeks, and led him to the doors of the church. They all had survival stories, and I thought, "This is so beautiful." I loved them all immediately. I felt very happy to be spending the day there. We laughed and joked and everyone called me "Baby Girl."

So I mopped and cleaned the kitchen, which was filled with old cooking and food-prep equipment that had been donated. All the food for lunch had been donated too, and it was pretty basic: Hot dogs, day-old bread, and gigantic cans of pork and beans. We prepared everything as lovingly as we could, and at noon, hundreds of people appeared out of nowhere and were waiting in line. I was astounded. *Where did all these people come from?* It was a cold, foggy San Francisco day and the wind was blowing, so people were bracing themselves against the side of the church and shivering. My job was to scoop the beans on to each Styrofoam plate as people walked by. I was smiling the whole time, thinking: *Here I am! I'm excited, I'm serving!* But everyone seemed really sad. They had their heads down, and nobody looked me in the eyes. I was struck by that.

The line just kept coming. At one point I took a break and went outside, and I noticed there were still people lined up way down the street. Eventually, we started running out of food and had to ration the portions. Instead of two hot dogs, two pieces of bread, and two scoops of beans, people got only one of each. People kept coming, some with kids, their clothes in tatters and their hair uncombed, and they got less and less food. Pretty soon the cook came out and said, "Half a hot dog, half a piece of bread, and one small scoop of beans." Then, with many people still waiting in line, we ran out of food. At that moment, almost everybody disappeared as quickly as they had come. A few stayed, though, and I watched them for a long time.

Later that afternoon, after we cleaned up, I went out to the curb and started sobbing. "This is not right!" I thought. What struck me most was how deeply I cared. I cared that people didn't get food. I cared about the children with holes in their jackets. I cared that it was cold, and I wondered where they went after waiting in line, what their life was like. It was gut-wrenching for me, an awakening moment, because I realized I could care about and love people I didn't even know. I'd never experienced that before; it was a very powerful feeling. I had seen people in my neighborhood suffering, but there was something about the number of people and the need for something as basic as food. My heart opened, and somehow I changed. I discovered that I cared deeply, that I wanted to alleviate suffering. I worked at Glide for a few more weeks and had a similar experience each time; and then I went back to my thirteen-year-old life. But something deep in me was touched; the seed of compassion had been watered.

Compassion is a powerful emotion that arises from deep within the heart in response to pain. It can arise in response to our own pain or in response to the suffering of those around us. What is challenging about this emotion is that we aren't powerful enough to completely take the pain of others away, so what is asked of us is to be present. Often I can't change a situation but what I can do is offer my sincere care and my loving presence. Author Leo Buscaglia was asked to judge a contest to find the most caring child. The winner was a four-year old whose neighbor had lost his wife. Upon seeing the elderly man cry, the little boy went into the man's yard, climbed onto his lap, and just sat there. When the boy's mother asked what he said to the neighbor, the boy replied, "Nothing, I just helped him cry."[2]

Thousands of US soldiers have returned from Iraq suffering from serious post-traumatic stress disorder (PTSD). A former University of California nurse in San Diego trained therapy dogs to help these traumatized veterans. Among the most debilitating symptoms of PTSD are the nightmares and night terrors that keep individuals reliving terrifying memories all night long. Over time, sleep deprivation becomes physically and emotionally destabilizing.

The first dogs were sent to soldiers who had the most debilitating symptoms and weren't responding to prescription medication; they were desperate, overwhelmed, and often suicidal. The dogs were trained to stay up during the night, and when a soldier was having a nightmare, the dog would reach out its paw and tap directly on the soldier's chest. Then it would lick his face. Feeling the tapping motion, the veteran would wake up and reorient himself. Receiving a compassionate response in moments of distress is what we all need. The veterans who received the dogs are doing much better and the results have astounded everyone.

In my twenties I began teaching a meditation program in Bay Area juvenile halls. We would go into the different units and teach a one-hour mindfulness class. I would do the majority of my work in the boys' units and I loved it. Most of the youth there were from Oakland. They held the youngest and the smallest kids in a separate area, so I began visiting that unit every Thursday night. There was a little boy in there who I fell in love with as soon as I laid eyes on him. He couldn't have been more than twelve and his name was Marcus. He had these huge brown eyes and the sweetest smile with dimples. Sometimes the younger kids had a harder time meditating. They would giggle and make fart sounds when everyone closed their eyes. We would all just laugh and then come back to feeling our breath again. But Marcus was a pro and he loved my class. He was very mature for his age, definitely an old soul. Every Thursday he was so excited to see me. I would always give him a huge hug and he would have the biggest smile on his face for the entire class.

After a while, I started to ask him more about his story. I came to find out his mother died when he very young and his father was a homeless man who was living on the streets. Nobody would take him in so he wound up in an abusive foster home that he ran away from. His social worker was unable to find him a new placement primarily because he was an older African American boy. Black boys tend to be the ones who languish and suffer the most in the foster care system. His social worker brought him to juvenile detention while she looked for another home, and sadly one day turned into eight months. I couldn't believe it. He hadn't done anything wrong and he was being treated like a criminal. He was all alone and scared. The love I started to develop for this kid was growing every day.

Every week I inquired, "When's your social worker coming to see you?" His only response was "I haven't seen her in weeks. I don't know what's going on. I don't know where I'm going to go." Many of the kids had similar stories. They had all been abandoned a long time ago, and I started to see my role not so much as a meditation teacher but more as a mother. At the end of my classes, the kids would all begin standing in a line and I would hug each child and remind them of how precious they were. The staff would just stare at me with shocked looks on their faces, They were amazed because these were kids who they labeled as violent and dangerous. I felt so much compassion for them and every week it was getting harder and harder to leave Marcus there. I wanted to adopt him; I wanted to adopt them all really. Then one day it happened. I came in to teach the class and he was gone. He had disappeared into the system, had gone off into the world by himself. I cried all the way home that night praying that Marcus would find the safe place he deserved. I don't think I will ever forget that kid. Man, he blasted my heart wide open.

I wanted others to see what I was experiencing. So I invited a friend, Alex Katz, who wrote for the Oakland Tribune, to come with me. He brought a photographer. He wrote an article with photos of me doing yoga and hugging the kids. It was a beautiful story and helped bring attention to our project and the kids. He said, "My heart is really changed watching you in here. I had so many ideas about who these kids were or what they needed. And you're right: it's just love and attention on some level." I responded, "Yeah. They all need our compassion."

When I try to suppress difficult emotions or act them out, it only amplifies my problems. By "difficult" emotions I mean grief, fear, rage and doubt or some variation of them. What I have learned is that the wisest response is to *feel* what is going on and stay present with myself. It can be so hard because we will do anything not to feel painful emotions. Distracting myself from facing my emotions unfortunately doesn't change them. Once the distraction is over, the emotions arise again. We are all learning how to stay present and this is what self-compassion is all about. The more you meet the suffering in you with love, the more you can be there for others. Staying present with our own pain takes a fierce heart, but we don't do it alone; we bring compassion with us.

A few years ago, I was completely exhausted from all the projects I was involved in, and I began to crave solitude. I have always felt that deep down I am secretly a nun and my yogini nature loves solitude. I have always saved money and structured my life simply so that I can travel and at certain times go on long retreats. So this time I planned a five-month retreat in Crestone, Colorado, an area at the foot of the Sangre de Cristo Mountains, sacred to Native American communities. I felt drawn to this place and had dreams that the land was calling me. Crestone is a hub of spiritual activity, with communities of many traditions that offer retreats and other programs.

I planned to spend the whole time at a Tibetan meditation center focusing on "purification practices"—prostrations, mantras, meditation, and visualizations. But after I'd been there for two months, a nun told me about a magical cabin way up in the mountains nearby, and I instantly knew I needed to spend the rest of my time on retreat there. I grew up in cities and am not that nature-ish, although I longed to be so; and this would be a real immersion in the natural world. So, despite snowstorms and freezing weather, up the mountain I went.

My cabin had a small solar panel, so I had a tiny fridge and lights for a couple of hours in the evening. There was a wood-burning stove, and when I got cold, I went out and got wood to make a fire. The caretaker brought food and water up every ten days, and I would meet him halfway up the rutty road. That was my only human contact. I decided against having a cell phone, and there was no Internet connectivity. I wanted to meditate like a true yogi. So there I was in this very isolated cabin, with an outhouse, a propane burner, a cushion, an altar, and a few Dharma books.

When I'd first heard about the cabin from the nun, I envisioned my retreat as a series of beautiful moments connecting with the Earth, with no one around to distract me. I imagined long periods of blissed out meditation. Setting up the space, though, I began to have second thoughts. Still, I encouraged myself, "Spring, you're here! You know the Dharma; it's time to rely on yourself. If times get hard, you can be your own refuge." I thought the worst that could happen would be a feeling, that is that I would have to *feel* something. "Okay," I thought, "I'll feel whatever comes up. I can do this!"

But the moment the caretaker got in his truck and headed back down the hill, I instantly plummeted into the most painful sorrow I've ever known. Oceans of tears interrupted by overwhelming terror. Every day tears poured down my cheeks, my chest ached, and my body was filled with grief. I started sobbing in the morning and it went on for hours, in waves. It was huge and kept getting bigger; I didn't understand where it was coming from. It was as though ten thousand years of ancestral sorrow was coming straight through my heart, and so I called it "African grief." It consumed me physically, mentally, and spiritually for hours, a kind of purification. I had co-led several grief rituals led by my dear friend Sobonfu Somé, a healer, teacher, and shaman from Burkina Faso in West Africa. She'd describe this grief that was far beyond anyone's control. She said that in her tradition, it's critical to feel it completely and then let it go. While I was wailing, it would turn into gospel hymns, screaming for hours, and witnessing my body contort in unimaginable positions. I thought I was going crazy, but I began to try to trust the process.

In the evenings, as it got dark outside, terror would grip my heart and I'd shake uncontrollably. I was an African American woman completely alone in a place populated by rednecks, I thought. I was sure I'd be attacked and killed at any moment, ripped to shreds by wild animals or deranged rednecks. I heard things moving outside in the dark, and I remember thinking, "This grief, terror, despair, and loneliness are too much. I'm not going to survive this experience." All day I cried, and at night I was on super-high alert. I kept trying to calm myself, "You live in East Oakland. That's way more dangerous than here. Actually, there's nobody around." But the fears and the energy I was releasing were primal, and rational considerations had no impact on this raw emotion. With endless grief and nightly terror, I hit my breaking point.

I began marking off the days on a calendar, knowing that one day it would all come to an end. It was then I realized how much I needed compassion. I needed to care for myself through this, I needed to help myself. So I began to meditate on self-care and self-compassion for hours at a time, holding my hands on my heart. I began doing prostrations and bowing before my altar for hours, taking refuge in Quan Yin, the bodhisattva of compassion. I began praying for compassion, I sang songs about compassion, and I chanted *Om Mani Padme Hum,* the great compassion mantra, constantly. I called in all the compassionate deities from Quan Yin to Mother Mary and everyone in between to help me meet this profound pain, realizing that without compassion, I would not be able to stay present with the powerful forces that were moving through me.

On the days I felt my compassion run out, I borrowed some from Green Tara. I would say, "Tara, please help me. I need some compassion. I've lost all of mine." And it would come. Then I'd say, "Thank you, I feel restored." I thought about all the people in that very moment meditating, going into churches and temples, praying and reflecting, all the monks and nuns all over the world, as well as all the laypeople. I knew that in some way I was connected to them, and that their practice and faith affect me. We're all interconnected.

The only way I could get any sleep was to stuff pillows behind me. I would sink down into them and imagine they were the giant bosoms of Mother Earth. I would imagine these big black arms reaching around me as if I were being held in the arms of the Great Mother, and I discovered that you can evoke compassion, this great force, and it will protect you.

After a month of this intense experience, I could feel that I was freeing myself of ancient suffering and that's when I recognized compassion as a great chief. He, She, They, It, whatever it is, when it showed up, it never left my side. With compassion, I was able to bear what felt unbearable. All I could do was feel the emotions and have faith that my heart was strong enough to take it. I thought about all the beings who throughout the ages had freed their minds through struggles. I thought of Dr. King and Harriet Tubman a lot, as well as Buddha and his great struggle with the demon Mara. I thought of Jesus and his forty days and forty nights in the desert, when they say he battled the devil, and all the nuns I'd read about, staying in hermitages and caves. I pictured all these epic sagas and thought, "If they could do it, I can do it. They had a mind just like mine. They suffered just as I'm suffering." I took comfort in the awareness that there are awakened beings all over the planet, and I was able to draw strength from the thought of their courage.

When we're purifying ourselves, when we're letting go of ancestral sorrows, it doesn't necessarily come with bliss and light. I had expected serenity and moments connecting to nature. I had imagined it would be all beauty. We want liberation; we want to be awakened. We want to understand the Four Noble Truths without feeling the suffering or anything else too difficult.[3] But that's not how it happens. Buddha himself went through a lot in his six years as an ascetic in the forest. He must have shed many tears, and he almost died from extreme deprivation. It was an epic battle. Christian mystics would build hermitages in the desert to do retreats, and they would be out there howling and screaming, and when someone would pass by, they would say, "It's just me and my mind." In the end, it's just you and your own mind, moment to moment. The only wise response is love and compassion.

This solo retreat was the most intense unraveling I've ever experienced. It was a three-month vision quest, and on this journey it was as if I'd died and been reborn. I look back on it with amazement that I endured something that difficult by myself. But in fact I was never alone; the great chief of compassion was by my side every day. We don't know what we'll have to go through. Spending three months by myself in that tiny cabin, I developed an unshakeable faith. At the beginning, I thought, "The worst that could happen is feeling." And wow, did I ever feel! Who knows where this stuff comes from? It was unwinding a sorrow so deep and a fear so entrenched that it felt it would break me at times. Without knowing it, I had prepared for years to be able to meet that experience and to begin to understand about the power of compassion.

When I was thirteen, doing community service at Glide Memorial Church, I had "signed on" somewhere really deep inside. I wanted to be a helper then, and I still do now. What touched me the most was that I saw suffering up close, and for the first time in my young life I saw compassion. This was what excited me about Glide; they were love and compassion in action and I felt it. That quality of love, when fully manifest, becomes the unbreakable lamp that we carry in the darkest of times. There are angels and frontline workers all over the world, all kinds of people who show up for others. I trust compassion, and I have come to know that without a doubt that it's the most powerful quality that our hearts posses. To live my life dedicated to alleviating my suffering and the suffering in this world is my joy. When people ask me what I do for fun I have to laugh; it's usually something having to do with compassion. We are never alone: the chief is always there.

Tenderly I now touch all things, knowing one day we will part.

—ST. JOHN OF THE CROSS

CHAPTER TEN

# HELLO/GOODBYE

MANY YEARS AGO, a friend and I decided to take a break from the busyness of our crazy lives and go on a mini-retreat, combining meditation with time in nature. At that time I was living in a lively community in the Haight-Ashbury district of San Francisco. It was a very chaotic yet transformative period in my life. We borrowed a friend's cabin located in a beautiful forest in nearby Mendocino. On our first day, we got up early, went outside, and began doing sitting and walking meditation. After several hours of meditating I casually glanced up and saw my friend walk by and suddenly it came to me: "*Hello. Goodbye. We are together now, and one day we'll both be gone.*" I mean really gone. I looked up at the trees, listened to the birds chirping and the insects buzzing, and realized *all* of this will be gone some day. I felt as though I understood in every cell of my mind and body, "This man is my dear friend, and yet one day we will part." The statement is obvious, of course, but the clarity and depth with which I experienced it were not ordinary. It was an insight into impermanence that broke my heart wide open.

Bear with me. Imagine something truly obvious you thought you understood—when suddenly the veil is lifted and you really *get* it. I envisioned my childhood friends, my grandmother, and every person I'd ever known, and it was all: Hello. Goodbye. Every moment is "hello," and then the inevitable "goodbye." I sat motionless, in silence, as though time had stopped while this truthful insight went so deep into my bones and my heart that I could barely contain it. My eyes flooded with tears and I was shaking. Everything was appearing and disappearing moment by moment. I was seeing the truth of life on such a deep level that all I could do was get on my knees and bow to it. So that's what I did.

I tried to share what was happening with my friend, but was unable to express the depth of the experience. So he looked at me like, "Right, I get it," and he just smiled and nodded his head. For several days after our retreat I wandered around Golden Gate Park like a mystic on the banks of the Ganges River in India, with tears flowing down my cheeks. Every time I saw a flower, a dog, a child, the sun—anything!—I would remember, "Hello. Goodbye." I phoned my mom and tried to explain how everything is impermanent and everyone needed to understand Hello, Goodbye; she paused for a moment, then laughed at me.

I went on experiencing Hello, Goodbye with everything, appreciating the profundity of impermanence even when letting go was painful. We're here, and then we disappear. Hello, Goodbye to long relationships, jobs, families, our bodies, trees, everything. There's no use clinging to anything; it's all temporary. I saw how our lives are just movies and every movie, no matter how much we love it, eventually comes to an end; it has to. Everything is in a state of change. Nothing is meant to last. It felt like my heart was exploding every moment. I couldn't figure out how to live with this new understanding. A door had opened and I saw something I needed to see. Then as suddenly as the insight had arisen, things slowly shifted and my mind went back to normal. I was actually overjoyed when it all went back to normal because I wasn't ready to live with seeing Hello/Goodbye in every moment. It had been an emotional roller coaster. I slowly went back to living my life in a familiar way again, but on a very deep level, the experience changed me.

Insights are the *"Aha"* and *"I get it"* moments that transform our lives. Insights happen when we see the truth in a way that pierces us. We can have a huge insight that shifts our whole perspective in an instant or we can have small insights that slowly chop away at our delusions one by one. *Aha!* moments continue to impact us, even after the momentary glimpse of truth wears off. And sometimes, as Zen Master Shunryu Suzuki explains, it's like walking through the mist. You don't realize it, but after a while you notice you're soaking wet. Impermanence is at the core of every great teaching. To see the truth of impermanence directly and clearly leads us on to the path of letting go. Letting go is the opposite of clinging; and holding on is the root of suffering. Everything comes down to this: Can you let go?

Awaken your fierce heart and try to understand that everything in this life is only temporary. We are impermanent, this moment is impermanent, this book is impermanent, your body is impermanent, and everything else about this human experience is impermanent. Like a flash of lightning in the sky, we appear, we dance, we disappear. It's part of the great mystery; it's part of this incredible journey, and we are all in it together. The truth is, all things are in a state of flux and they eventually cease to exist because everything has an expiration date. It's impossible to hold on to anything. Why, you ask? Because in life everything is always changing; that's its nature. It's very important to let this truth sink in over and over. The only thing you can count on in life is *change.*

There's no doubt that were living in a time of unimaginable change. The environment, political situations, whole systems are collapsing right before our eyes. Prepare yourself: we have collectively entered the eye of the storm; the birth of something new is upon us. Ecologists, scholars, wisdom keepers, and indigenous leaders have dubbed this time "The Great Turning." This term has been popularized by the work of Buddhist teacher and deep ecologist Joanna Macy. In systems theory, any time a great shift is underway, we enter a period of chaos right before the whole system collapses. This is just a stage, however it can be a scary one if we are attached and holding on to anything. Things are getting better and better, worse and worse, and faster and faster at the same time. This pressure is causing everything to move at lightning speed. To say that this is a transformative period would be an understatement. As we know, sometimes the endings of things can be painful, overwhelming, and even violent. In the final hours, an insane grasping takes over; it's a futile attempt to hold on to that which is inevitably going to change. Your wisdom, courage, and strength are needed now more than ever.

I have slowly recognized that everything is constantly moving, flowing, and shifting. It's a river that always flows back to the ocean. There is a loving intelligence behind everything and it's moving us all through stages rhythmically. Periods of expansion and growth are often followed by periods of contraction; as the universe moves and dances we inevitably shift and dance as well. Nothing stays still for long and everything is alive and moving through phases and cycles. Our inner cycles and the outer cycles are connected because when one shifts it causes the others to shift as well. It's easier to be aware of this when we're able to spend time in nature.

We can see cycles of change in our own lives. From the time we are born until we die, we are moving through phases and cycles of life—being a baby, then a child, the turbulent years of adolescence, and the stages of adulthood, then old age. Everything is arising and passing. Everything in nature is born and then dies. These are the cycles of life and everything has a beginning, middle, and ending. We can see the seasons change a leaf, from the time it grows until it falls from the tree and returns to the earth. The summer and winter solstices mark the shortest and longest days of the year. Flowers bloom, and then they're gone. Days come and go. To live with real freedom and to let go is to understand the temporary and cyclical nature of life.

There are huge Earth and planetary cycles such as the rotation of the Earth around the sun, a cycle that takes 365 days. It takes the sun approximately 225–250 million years to complete one journey around the galaxy's center. This amount of time—the time it takes us to orbit the center of the galaxy—is sometimes called a "cosmic year." As mind-boggling as that seems, we can see these rhythmic cycles operating everywhere all the time. Throughout all of theses various cycles, what is at the heart of it all is the continuous experience of impermanence.

Many ancient cultures attached great importance to astronomical events and taught ways to interpret and understand the cycles they observed. In astrology, the Egyptians, Tibetans, and ancient Mayans developed elaborate systems based on the movements of the sun, moon, and planets to predict various phases. In 2012 there was a lot of talk about the Mayan calendar and its ending date. The Mayan prophecy fascinated people because it was another symbolic representation of the ending and beginning of a new period of time. Over the years many people have written and commented about seven year cycles and the profound shifts that seem to occur in seven-year intervals. In Hindu tradition, cyclical periods of time are referred to as Yugas. In the Buddhist cosmology it is taught that we are living in a great period of time referred to as an aeon. Most people don't notice these cyclical changes and are completely unaware of the fact that from the micro levels to the macro levels everything is constantly changing.

The Buddha told us that we can't cling to something that's changing. We want steadiness. We want "Hello, hello, hello" forever. Or maybe we want "Goodbye, goodbye, goodbye." Whichever side we're on, things arise and pass, independent of our feelings of wanting and not wanting. It drives us crazy because the truth is we have no control. We might prefer to say hello only to things that make us happy; but that's not an option. As wisdom grows, we see that we can't control life's unpredictability, no matter how hard we try. People who crave control have the hardest time on this path because the whole journey is about letting go. Ajahn Chah, the great Thai meditation master, taught, "Do everything with a mind that lets go. Don't accept praise or gain or anything else. If you let go a little, you will have a little peace; if you let go a lot, you will have a lot of peace; if you let go completely, you will have complete peace."[1]

Most human beings hate the idea of impermanence; in actuality we deny it, fight it, and cling to everything. In the West, we deny the reality of change and we look for stability in places where it can never be found. Pema Chödrön says, "We are like people in a boat that is falling apart trying to hold on to the water."[2] We want things to last forever and we suffer when they don't. We experience anger primarily because we feel deeply hurt and an overwhelming sense of loss and betrayal when things change. We may keep asking the question, "Why is life doing this to me?" A project we enjoyed working on is over; now it no longer exists. We think: "I am a good person. Why did that happen to me?" Why, why, why? The answer is always "It's just the way things are." It can feel as if everything is against us and we become upset, disillusioned, and angry at life.

There is both a hard and a soft aspect to everything.. The hard aspect is that we don't want our lives to change and inevitably they do. When the man I loved wanted to marry someone else, it was gut wrenching for me. I couldn't believe it; but once again I had to except that in an instant everything can change. It's hard because sometimes life can be so beautiful, and at other times so painful; it's truly a wild ride. Infinite possibilities surround us. Everything is always dying and always being born. It can make us feel sad, excited, and hopeful at the same time. We'll always experience a certain amount of stress due to things changing. However we don't have to suffer so much when we understand that this is just the way things are.

The soft aspect of impermanence is that no matter how difficult something is at this moment, rest assured it will pass. No emotion, no suffering, no situation, no person lasts forever, eventually, sooner or later, it will change. Jarvis Jay Masters has this insight into his time in prison: "Understanding impermanence, that things are here today and gone tomorrow, really helps. No matter how bad something is, you can remind yourself, 'Damn, this won't last.' Then when it doesn't last, you can laugh and say, 'I knew it.'"[3]

The soft side also embodies the spirit of freedom, and challenges our ideas of destiny. We can become courageous and take bold leaps. All things are possible.

I have also come to see that any time we make a change, there's grief on some level. When moving from one step to the next, whether it's calling in something new or leaving a job or a relationship— even if what we're leaving is toxic, abusive, agonizing, it's often painful to say goodbye. Even when people overcome addiction, they can experience great sorrow in saying goodbye to their drug of choice. Any time we make a change, we experience a small death. When we shed things, we often get confused because even as we celebrate the change, we sometimes still feel sadness. "Well, I *wanted* this," we might say to ourselves. "So why is there sorrow?" The sorrow we feel is the sadness of letting go of an energetic part of ourselves that has died. It's the grief of shifting out of one situation and flowing into another. Sometimes we even have to let go of an old identity or sense of self. Our old identity, even if dysfunctional and painful, is also an old friend. Like shoes we've worn a long time but that are too small, we've been through a lot together. We keep wearing those shoes because we like them—even if they rub our feet, they're familiar. Then one day we just get rid of them and we experience some sorrow—the loss of letting go. If you ask the universe, "Give me liberation, I want to be free," then you can't take all the junk you have accumulated with you. We have to choose between freedom and our junk, and it's not always an easy choice.

Letting go of people is a painful reality that all human beings experience. When we try to hold on to relationships that are ending, the suffering can become unbearable. People come together, form a relationship, move in together, and in one way or another, at some time they say goodbye. Perhaps the relationship just fails, something else emerges, this or that happens. That's the nature of reality, and clinging doesn't stop the process. My teacher Joseph Goldstein used to tell me, "Clinging is rope burn." It's painful when you hang on; you have to let go eventually. Please understand that you haven't done anything wrong when things end. It's the nature of life itself. It feels personal but it's not. Again and again you must remind yourself, *this is just the way things are.*

In Buddhist cosmology the universe is ruled over by Yama, the lord of death. He is always depicted as a terrifying-looking demon with huge fangs and claws. In many paintings he is holding the entire universe in his hands with his giant mouth open, waiting to take a bite. Like sand in an hourglass, the grains of our life are slowly dropping, one by one. Whether you feel you have a lot of time or never enough, you're being pulled downstream by invisible forces. We don't know how much time we have left and it's shocking to see the years fly by. Just as we were born, we will pass away. Death is certain; only the time of death is unknown. In actuality we're not that different from rainbows. We make an appearance, and we don't know when we'll be gone. For some, death seems terrifying. Others see death as an essential part of life's journey, a state of grace.

We see death constantly in the news and all around us, but when somebody we love dies, it's painful to accept. People share stories with me about the profound shifts that take place after the death of a loved one. Over the years I have worked with so many people who have lost loved ones unexpectedly, some through murders, others in car accidents, or because of physical illnesses. Even if someone has died peacefully of old age, it still shocks us. It still hurts. Up-close encounters with death shake us out of the dream state of everyday existence and we start to pay attention!

Death is the ultimate teacher on impermanence and it's the one thing we can all count on. We have to come face-to-face with this truth and reflect on what we want to do with our most precious resource, and that is our time. To use our time meaningfully is very important now. We don't know when our time will be to leave this world. This is a huge, powerful insight. We can't control what happens in the outer world, but we can choose how we live our life right now.

It's all so incredibly deep, this human experience; it always brings tears to my eyes. The cactus flowers that bloom once in a century won't last all that long, but I appreciate them anyway. I am learning how to love the things that are fleeting, like rainbows and butterflies, as well as the things that seem like they'll be around forever, like giant redwood trees, and mountains. They're all a beautiful expression of themselves, and I can enjoy them while they're present and honor their memory when they're gone.

When you start to listen to your heart, to your inner voice, a big doorway opens. It's up to you whether to step through. We've got to choose. We want to be free, but we don't want to let go of anything. That's a problem. Sometimes the boat we're on is not taking us where we're supposed to go, and we let go, or it lets us go. Either way, that particular boat ride is now over. We're in a new cycle that's part of our life's journey, a pivot point, a launching pad, the time when the changes we've longed for get made. Sometimes, there's no going back. The ball is rolling. The Buddha encouraged us to know the sweet joy of living the Way. He is referring to a presence so deep that we are open to the mystery of everything shifting and changing.

Wise love understands that everything appears at certain times in order to help us grow, and then they disappear at the exact moment they're supposed to. To live with wisdom means to know that things are always changing and that there's great power in acceptance. Our task is to embrace everything and everyone with our whole heart, while understanding that the nature of life is change. It's a paradox, but this is the path of the warrior. The truth will set us free, but it's sometimes brutal to take. We're being pushed through the small eye of the needle toward this truth in every moment. Even as you read, this paper is yellowing, the words are fading, your understanding is growing or diminishing. All things—a flower's beauty, the sunset's glory—are changing.

What's next? Don't know. Let's go. Hello/Goodbye.

"The Dakini Speaks" by Jennifer Welwood

My friends, let's grow up.
Let's stop pretending we don't know the deal here.
Or if we truly haven't noticed, let's wake up and notice.
Look: Everything that can be lost, will be lost.
It's simple—how could we have missed it for so long?
Let's grieve our losses fully, like ripe human beings,
But please, let's not be so shocked by them.
Let's not act so betrayed,
As though life had broken her secret promise to us.

Impermanence is life's only promise to us,
And she keeps it with ruthless impeccability.
To a child she seems cruel, but she is only wild,
And her compassion exquisitely precise:
Brilliantly penetrating, luminous with truth,
She strips away the unreal to show us the real.
This is the true ride—let's give ourselves to it!
Let's stop making deals for a safe passage:
There isn't one anyway, and the cost is too high.
We are not children anymore.
The true human adult gives everything for what
cannot be lost.
Let's dance the wild dance of no hope!⁴

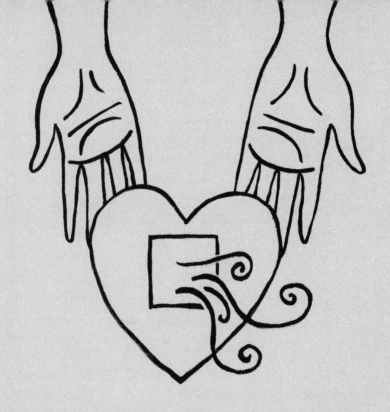

Resentment is like drinking poison and then hoping it
will kill your enemies.

—NELSON MANDELA

## CHAPTER ELEVEN

# FREE YOUR HEART

I HAVE BEEN BLESSED OVER THE YEARS to have encountered many beautiful saints and several powerful demons. The saints have shown me by their living example that forgiveness is possible, but it's been the demons that have challenged me to put everything I hold sacred into practice. That is what demons are for; they sometimes appear in disguises, and at other times they appear clearly labeled, offering us an invitation on to the dark path for a period of time. In whatever manifestation or form they take, what they offer us is the bitterest medicine and the hardest lessons. Like a metal sword being crafted in hot coals, our own strength is also forged through the fires of hell. Inevitably what we learn from all demons is how to love, how to forgive, and how to reclaim our own power.

As an African American woman, practicing forgiveness keeps me from being consumed by anger. People die from hatred. I beg you not to become one of them. Forgiving everyone for everything is my only practice these days. The heart wants to be free and the only way is by letting go of the resentments we carry from the past. This chapter is deeply personal and was difficult to write, but you'll discover that my stories are familiar ones. I have nothing new to say because we all know these truths in our bones. These are the struggles of our people and the struggle of humankind.

My Tibetan teacher Mingier Rinpoche would always say, "Be thankful for your enemies. They teach you everything about compassion and patience." To be thinking of people who have done great harm in that way is a radical shift. We can use painful experiences to evoke compassion. César Chávez, who endured so much while leading the farm workers movement said, "We draw our strength from the very despair in which we have been forced to live. We shall endure."[1] My journey into forgiveness has always been about enduring.

At the age of twenty-four, after twenty-one years of separation, I was reunited with my biological father. I only had two clear memories of him and I cherished both of them. I remember once when he took me to get some ice cream. He was smiling at me as I sat in the front seat of his car, licking a gigantic vanilla ice cream cone. The other vivid memory is of him popping in unexpectedly one night to pay us a visit. I jumped straight onto his lap and, feeling so happy to see him, I wrapped my tiny arms around his neck. When it came time for him to go, I cried and begged him to stay. I hid his hat to keep him from leaving, but he found it and headed out the door again. He was always leaving.

I genuinely missed him throughout my life; his absence had a deep impact on me. My mother would describe him as an unstable, selfish man who had abandoned us. I remember moving in with my mother's new boyfriend, who would tell me over and over how my father never cared about me. I think that was the hardest thing to accept. I had one tiny Polaroid photograph of him, and I would gaze at it and make up elaborate fantasies that he would pick me up from school one day and take me on a magical adventure. Deep down, I wondered if he ever thought about me at all, but he was always on my mind. When a parent disappears from your life, there's a deep sense of loneliness, a wound in your heart. I never knew what to believe about his whereabouts and, as the years went by, I finally gave up all hope of ever seeing him again.

I was thinking about all of this during the long flight my mother, sister, and I took from San Francisco to Philadelphia. My grandmother—my father's mother—had invited us to attend Uncle Wayne's birthday party. It was also a family reunion, to be held at a big park in Wilmington, Delaware. We had always stayed in touch with my father's family on the East Coast—my grandparents, four uncles, two aunts, and dozens of cousins. My father's people were a hundred percent old-school African Americans with deep Southern Baptist roots. Everything revolved around my grandmother; She was a generous and loving woman, the matriarch of the family. Her home was the gathering place for every special occasion.

Over the years, my mother kept in touch by sending her letters and school photos, and in turn my grandmother would send us cookies and Christmas cards. When I was thirteen, we visited for the first time, and our whole East Coast family warmly embraced us. Since most of my mother's family was deceased, my mom, sister, and I were like orphans, and in my grandmother's arms we felt at home.

My father's whereabouts were unknown for many years, and not just to us; he had also been out of contact with his own family for years. At one point, they didn't know if he was alive or dead. Then out of the blue, he called his family and announced he was coming home. Everyone rose to the occasion to greet him. Some helped with plane tickets, others with housing. My uncle even offered him a job. My father left Arizona, and returned to his hometown of Wilmington, Delaware, bringing his four young children with him.

After we landed in Philadelphia, my father and grandmother pulled up in an old car. My mother, sister, and I stood outside baggage claim. My father immediately jumped out of the driver's seat and yelled, "California Love!" at the top of his lungs, then burst out laughing. Our eyes met for the first time in twenty-one years, and I cracked up laughing too. His laughter was a way to break the tension of such an epic occasion. I had thought about this exact moment for so long, it felt weird and strangely familiar, even after twenty-one years.

The following days were filled with sadness, laughter, confusion, and love. It was difficult to know what to share; we were catching up on a lifetime. There were conflicting stories between my parents about what had happened and whose fault it was. When we moved from southern to northern California, my mother didn't leave an address or phone number, she was so angry with him. My father said I was always in his heart and that he always loved me. I came to see that he wasn't the hero I had imagined, nor the villain others believed him to be. As I looked into his eyes, I felt deep compassion and forgiveness. I saw the suffering he carried and understood that he was just a human being trying to figure out how to be happy.

In truth it was easy to have compassion and forgiveness in that moment; my father's life was in complete shambles. He was the single parent of four active, young boys, and he was dedicated to raising them. For that, I applauded him. His wife, the boys' mom, was a crack cocaine addict and prostitute living on the streets most of the time. He did whatever he could to help her recover, and when she was diagnosed with AIDS, he decided to bring his family back to Delaware where he had grown up. He had very little money and he needed support.

Being reunited with my father didn't turn out to be the fantasy I had envisioned, but my life has never been a fairy tale. After seeing him, I forgave both of my parents. I knew that everything in my life had happened for a reason; there was no one to blame anymore. I understood why each of them had made the decisions they had made. As I flew back to California, there was a deep sense of peace and a feeling of closure.

To understand everything is to forgive everything; but how do we begin to forgive everything? How can we forgive genocide, racism, sexism, homophobia, colonization, and all the other ways human beings act out of greed, hatred, and delusion? Only someone with wisdom and a fierce heart can do that. A few years ago I had the good fortune of attending an event that included the viewing of an inspiring film about Garchen Triptrul Rinpoche. I got to meet him during the event and learn all about his life. He had been in a Chinese prison for twenty years and went through all kinds of the most brutal torture that you could imagine. When he got out of prison and went into exile in India, the Dalai Lama asked him, "Were you ever scared?" He replied, "I was only scared when I lost my compassion [for my torturers] for a little while." This story about his forgiveness—using the worst conditions to obtain profound freedom—is so inspiring to me and to countless others. There's something profoundly illuminated in his heart; you can feel it when he talks. He left prison with no PTSD, only love, compassion, and complete forgiveness toward everyone. Now he has started a large spiritual community in Arizona and has become a worldwide inspiration. He carries a spinning prayer wheel with him and turns it practically 24/7. "Millions of *mani* prayers, compassion prayers," he says. "I have to keep spinning it for the benefit of all beings."

When I was fifteen, powerful forces propelled me in a dangerous direction. My mother's abusive boyfriend made our home a living hell, and I felt I had no choice but to move out. A year later, during a peak period of violent gang activity in South Los Angeles when thousands of young men were joining the Crips and the Bloods,

I was living on my own in the midst of it all. I spent a lot of time around drug dealers, hustlers, and gang members, and got hurt countless times.

I saw how drugs, rage, and violence fuel urban war zones, and I was drawn into the confusion, danger, and the pain without understanding why. It took witnessing terrible violence, almost getting killed in a drive-by shooting, and nearly dying in a car accident to finally wake me up. These were the darkest years of my life, and I feel lucky to be alive. Many friends and acquaintances from that period were imprisoned, and others died tragically.

It was during that dark time that André appeared in my life. He was in his early twenties, a lifelong gangbanger and a drug dealer. He had grown up on the streets, his gang was his only family, and he was fiercely loyal. As a teenager, he'd been shot and beaten up many times, and his face and body had the scars to show for it. At age sixteen, I was no longer living with my mother. A friend and I shared a small apartment, and one of André's friends lived in the same building. To get by, I'd started selling small bags of marijuana. André and I became acquainted when I began buying large quantities of marijuana from him, then selling it for a profit. I never felt good about it doing it, but I had no job and had rent and other bills to pay.

I saw right away that he was dangerous and I felt afraid in his presence. Yet we had established a business relationship and I thought I was in control. Then he began to act obsessive around me and started to stalk me. I ignored my gut instincts and overlooked his behavior to keep my weed business going. Then one day, I was alone at a friend's house waiting for her and her boyfriend to return; André figured out where I was and showed up. I didn't want to let him in, but I did. Within minutes, he attacked and raped me. I fought with all my strength, but he was too strong. My legs were bruised and I was scared. When my friends returned, he threatened me. I was hurt and confused, so I stayed silent. For the next couple of months, he continued to stalk me, even kidnapping me once while I was outside my house. He forced me into his car and I endured a night of hell. Finally, he drove me home in the morning. He called me constantly, demanding that I be his girlfriend. I knew I was in danger and needed to leave. He knew where I lived, had my phone number, and was becoming more violent and erratic. Two days after the kidnapping, I packed my bags and moved away.

I knew André for just a short time, but it changed my life. Until then, I had been a free spirit and trusted everyone. After I moved away I blocked it all out, but much later in my life it all came up again. I relived everything in vivid detail and I began to do deep forgiveness work. When I heard later from a friend that André was in prison serving a twenty-five-year sentence for drug-related charges, I felt compassion for him.

In the Babemba tribe of South Africa, when a person acts irresponsibly or unjustly, he is placed in the center of the village, alone and unrestrained. All work ceases, and every man, woman, and child in the village gathers in a large circle around the accused. Then each person in the tribe speaks to him, one at a time, each recalling the good things the person in the center of the circle has done in his lifetime. Every incident, every experience that can be recalled accurately and in detail is recounted—all his positive attributes, good deeds, strengths, and kindnesses are recited carefully and at length. This tribal ceremony often lasts for several days. At the end, the tribal circle is broken, a joyous celebration takes place, and the person is symbolically and literally welcomed back into the tribe.

Forgiveness doesn't mean not standing up for what's right. It also doesn't mean not having boundaries. I forgave André, but that doesn't mean I want him to come over for dinner. Forgiveness doesn't mean we stop protecting others or speaking up when we can. It just means we aren't motivated by rage and hatred. "We're not punished for our anger, we're punished by it."[1] We can do our activist work by calling on the forces of truth and love. That is what we are *for*. We want a just world for all beings. We can transmute our anger into a cry for justice and it can become a much more powerful force. It becomes soul force that can move mountains and ignite great movements.

We must also have faith and remember that everyone can change, every human being has the potential to transform. Bryon Widner was known as an enforcer—someone hired to extort money through intimidation—for US racist groups and the founder of the Vinlanders skinhead gang in Ohio. Getting married and having a child radically changed him and opened his heart. He began rejecting the racist beliefs that had made him a notorious figure among America's extreme Right. However, he struggled to readapt to society because of the web of racist Nazi tattoos that covered his entire face and neck. He looked like a monster and his appearance frightened people. He had left the movement, created a good family life and felt he had so much to live for. With the help of loving people and support from anti-hate organizations, the former racist embarked on a series of twenty-five painful surgeries that took sixteen months and cost $32,400. "I was totally prepared to douse my face in acid," Bryon said. "I was that desperate to remove my tattoos." His painful physical transformation was just as incredible as his inner transformation. As the tattoos were being removed from his face, the hatred was being released from his heart. Bryon is now an advocate for civil rights.[3]

Learning how to forgive ourselves is also critically important. A big part of Bryon Widner's story was forgiving himself for everything he had done. I too did many things when I was younger that I wish I hadn't. I can't go back and change them, but I can commit to not repeating the same mistakes over and over. I've worked with many people who are struggling to forgive themselves for actions done in anger or confusion. Sometimes we need to engage in loving acts to purify past actions so that we can let go of them. I always encourage people to write letters to those they have hurt. Ask for forgiveness from those who you've harmed. Sometimes praying and doing charitable acts helps clear our consciousness so that we can move forward. Commit to living a different way; commit to living with heart.

The Buddha teaches, "Hatred never ceases by hatred but by love alone is healed. This is the ancient and eternal law."[4]

Nelson Mandela understood the power of forgiveness on many levels. He understood that before forgiveness can start, a truth and reconciliation process is needed. When he was released from prison after twenty-seven years and became President of South Africa, along with Archbishop Desmond Tutu and others he quickly set up the Truth and Reconciliation Commission, a powerful council that would hold tribunals and offer people pardon for crimes they had committed during the brutal years of apartheid.

Mandela abolished the apartheid system within moments after he was elected. However, the black community felt a deep vengeance for decades of abuse, murder, and injustice at the hands of the white government. It was a celebratory time, but also a dangerous one: the country could have been on the brink of a civil war, a powder keg ready to explode. A clear voice of wisdom and compassion was needed to address the horrors that had gone on for years. To help the nation come to grips with itself and what it had been through, the Truth and Reconciliation Commission began broadcasting on public television the cases it was hearing. To be granted a pardon, which meant basically appealing to the state for forgiveness, a person had to confess every act they had committed, honestly and clearly, giving names, dates, people involved, and each crime they had participated in, detailed to the extent they could remember. They also had to commit to never engaging in those actions again and apologize to the whole nation.

In the beginning, only black Africans came forward. But after the first year, many white police officers began to come before the tribunal, asking for forgiveness. The black community was riveted watching these proceedings every evening on public television. Each case was hotly debated and as the facts were uncovered, the topic of forgiveness was discussed in families throughout the country. Instead of thoughts of war and revenge, the whole country was forced to deal with the truth of injustice and the possibility of forgiveness. The hearings went on for years, and the cases were legendary. Even Winnie Mandela appeared before the tribunal asking for forgiveness. This process helped the nation come to grips with itself, and it allowed for healing, as people were asking for and receiving forgiveness.

Nelson Mandela's death in 2015 had a big impact on me, and his life, his legacy, and his message of forgiveness will live on forever, through me and all the people who remember him in the depths of our hearts.

The heart longs to be free and forgiveness is the direct pathway to that freedom. Without it we can never let others love us nor can we love others fully. We become like beautiful boats that are tied to the dock. The entire ocean awaits us when we are ready. We start our forgiveness process with ourselves in mind first. We do it for us. We do it to reclaim what we have lost, and we do it because it's the only thing that makes sense.

The Church says the body is a sin.
Science says the body is a machine.
Advertising says the body is a business.
The body says, "I am a fiesta."

**—EDUARDO GALEANO**

CHAPTER TWELVE

# YOUR TREE OF LIFE

As a culture we are just at the very beginning of understanding how much our bodies are involved in our overall healing process. The unfolding of our spiritual lives revolves around understanding who and what we are through the doorway of the body. We have so much to learn and our bodies have so much wisdom to share. I see the human body as a sacred tree of life because within it is contained all our personal DNA and the DNA of the entire universe. Essentially the body functions as a vast storehouse of information and a holder of our personal, collective, and cosmic histories. The roots of this tree go into infinity; the body is extraordinary in its abilities and magical in its processes.

The thoughts we think and the experiences we have shape the body and its energies. Our personal joys and traumas and even those of our ancestors are stored in our cells and expressed in our genes. Everything registers, everything is logged, every experience is counted, and nothing is ever left out. When we still our body and mind, we can feel the movements and the blocks within, and our past, present, and even our future can be revealed. Stories and experiences, difficulties and traumas can all be felt directly through the body. We can learn to release the heavy, painful, and dark energy we carry and learn how to access our innate wisdom.

The Buddha taught his disciples to be "mindful of the body *in* the body."[1] We can describe this as *embodiment,* or to "occupy the body," remembering the Occupy Movement that started in New York and spread to Oakland and many other cities. Like mindfulness practice, the intent of the Occupy Movement was liberation. We must learn how to occupy our own bodies and we start by understanding the different levels of the human system and how they affect our physical body.

# FOUR LEVELS OF THE HUMAN SYSTEM

## MENTAL LEVEL OF THE HUMAN SYSTEM

More and more as a culture we are learning how our thoughts and beliefs affect our overall mental and physical well-being. From the observations of the Eastern masters to the discoveries of modern-day neuroscience, the link between the mind and body is becoming undeniable. We are what we think, and our personal beliefs and biography literally become our inner biology. Prolonged patterns of negative thinking are the fuel for chronic depression and anxiety disorders, all of which have reached epidemic proportions in the West. Our inaccurate views and opinions about ourselves can and do create a very toxic environment within the heart and the mind.

Paying attention is the beginning of change. As we establish connection between body and mind, we enter new territory where there is potential for healing. All of our destructive mental habits arise and reveal themselves when we sit in meditation. Our mind goes through a very powerful cleansing process. As we get to the root of unhealthy patterns of thinking, buried memories, unconscious thoughts, and hidden issues reveal themselves so that we can face them and let them go. In meditation practice, we learn step by step how to transform the damaging mental patterns into healthy ones.

Applying awareness to the body, dwelling in the body, scanning the body—when in meditation we bring our loving awareness to each part of the body—all these practices interrupt the flow of our habitual negative thought patterns and have a healing effect. We're no longer glued to our inner television set: our thinking. Most of what's on our TV is terrible. It might be different if it was beautiful or fun, but mostly it's a horror story. Violence over and over; it's not only brutal on our mind but also on our body. When we apply awareness to the body, there is a healing effect on us as individuals, and we become happier and more connected to our real self.

Deep within us are other people's ideas, opinions, and prejudices, including what we most despise in others—racism, misogyny, homophobia, and more—leading us to feel disconnected and disempowered. As we meditate and learn to be present, a wise voice inside comes alive and starts to transform the places in us that are deeply confused. We learn to treat ourselves with respect, to listen to our bodies so that we can access a much deeper power. Through uniting our mind, body, and spirit, something happens. We start to hear the healthy part of the mind. This all begins when we allow ourselves to be present, to feel, and to listen.

## EMOTIONAL LEVEL OF THE HUMAN SYSTEM

Usually we think of our pain and our emotions as interfering with the process of looking deeply. Everything else is great, but not this: "this cannot be a part of Dharma, or part of me." The willingness to come face to face with our emotions is a big part of the journey within. To unlock the emotions that we have spent a lifetime suppressing or acting out, they all must be felt and understood with compassion. Everything in our storehouse has to be opened up—all the cupboards, all the closets. That's what we do on retreat. To free ourselves, we need to make peace with all the parts of ourselves. We've all had traumatic experiences. My own include abuse, abandonment, and rape at a young age. Our histories are buried under layers of self-protection and beneath the things society tells us we're not supposed to feel.

During one very long retreat, I woke up early in the morning with a pain so debilitating I couldn't move. I looked for my roommate, but she'd already left. It felt as if I were being stabbed again and again. As I lay there, memories of abuse began flooding my mind, and the sharp pain moved from my lower abdomen down into my vagina. I was sweating profusely, and the images, sensations, and feelings just kept coming. I was certain something was terribly wrong and that I would probably die. I wanted to call 911, but I couldn't move or speak. I began to pray and say my goodbyes to the world.

I tried to be present as these excruciating energies were coursing through me, reliving the trauma I'd undergone during each past painful experience, After an hour or two, seeing that I wasn't dying, my perspective began to shift from "this is a medical emergency" to recognizing it as a profound release. I started to feel compassion for my body. I could see it was crying out in distress. It was still impossible for me to move.

I saw that this was emotional pain I'd been holding for decades under layers of numbness, and it was expressing itself because I was ready. Until then, it would have been more than I could allow into awareness. Now I was able to stay present with the depths of pain in my abdomen, my genitals, and my heart. Hours passed and I continued to lie quietly, doing my best to pacify my fears and comfort my body. Finally, at almost midday, the pain began to subside, and I could stand up. For the next few days, I was exhausted and had difficulty walking. But I came through it, and as I released those traumas my emotional body began to feel more joyful and much more stable.

I've heard of similar experiences from others. One friend, who had been a serious heroin addict as a teenager, fell on the ground shaking and convulsing uncontrollably during a retreat. His physical addiction had long worn off, and now he was ready to feel the emotional trauma of being an addict and the circumstances that had brought it about. Another student I worked with, who had been involved in a sadomasochistic (BDSM) relationship at an early age, relived episodes of violence. His body contorted and stretched in positions similar to the ones he had experienced years earlier. He felt a lot of sadness as he relived those experiences. Our bodies hold everything. Sitting on the meditation cushion, our bodies can feel like they're in a war zone. People often experience extreme physical sensations during retreats. Vomiting, fevers, pain, and other intense physical experiences are not unusual. The body has its own natural intelligence and it knows how to heal itself, if we allow it to. It knows how to let go of the emotions that sometimes get stuck.

Another friend, who suffered from terrible migraines, relived a traumatic memory. She was late for school one morning, and her father hit her on the head with a belt buckle so hard that she bled uncontrollably. During meditation, the painful memory returned, and she sat with it, allowing all of her emotions to be felt. After that, the headaches she'd had for most of her life began to subside. A healing had taken place. These are all experiences of trauma re-expressing itself emotionally and physically, bringing up fear, grief, sorrow, and physical pain, and after that, relief. When trauma that has gone underground begins to surface, if we are in a safe place and it can express itself, we can be released from the effects of it.

I met Julie while I was teaching a three-month meditation course. An incredibly strong, wise woman, she had just passed the bar exam and came on retreat to heal and to discover her deeper purpose in life. She had been meditating for several years. Julie was of Puerto Rican descent, brought up in housing projects in the Bronx. She had overcome every obstacle presented to her and had an incredibly kind and compassionate heart. I enjoyed working with her during the retreat, and we became very close. One day, she came into a meeting crying as she shared what had happened the day before. She was practicing walking meditation indoors, going back and forth slowly, feeling her body moving and her feet touching the floor. There had been a snowstorm the night before, and it was bitter cold outside. On one side of the room, there was a wall heater and it was warm, and on the other side of the room it was very cold. As she walked mindfully, she could feel the heat warming her body as she walked toward the heater and experienced the sensations of coldness as she went to the other side of the room. This went on for some time.

At one point as she approached the heater, she began sobbing deeply, flooded by emotional memories of her childhood. When she was growing up, her family was unable to pay for heat, and they would crowd around the oven in the kitchen desperate to stay warm during the long New York winters. Her body, feeling the warmth of the wall heater, unlocked those painful emotions. She began shaking and sobbing uncontrollably as she stood in front of heater, allowing herself to feel the warmth. The emotions had been locked in her body. The sorrow of poverty and the struggles of the long winters without heat had taken their toll; she lovingly allowed herself to feel the pain and her body began to release waves of grief and despair. She stood in front of the heater for hours, feeling the comfort of the warmth her body had been deprived of all those years growing up. She was able to stay with the process, and she understood that something important was happening.

In Western culture, we tend to undermine the body's natural wisdom by diagnosing our feelings and then medicating ourselves.

Something's happening on the emotional level and we say, "Let's get rid of it." Mindfulness of feelings, *being* with them, *feeling* them in our body is the way to heal ourselves. Learning to be mindful when you feel rage, sorrow, and grief takes practice. We're not stopping our feelings or acting them out, we're just learning how to be present with them.

## PHYSICAL LEVEL OF THE HUMAN SYSTEM

Our society tries in various ways to convince us to hate our bodies, and some interpretations of religious teachings tell us to mistrust our bodies. I used to despise my body. It wasn't perfect, I thought. It didn't look the way I wanted. We judge ourselves by media standards. If you're brown, gender fluid, or you have a disability, it can be even more painful. We don't see our bodies as a sacred tree of life; we don't really value ourselves. "Don't get sick. Don't complain. Don't get all achy on me. Suck it up." We'll work twenty hours straight and expect no resistance from our body. That's brutal. And then it gets sick, and we're mad and ashamed to rest. Only in a crisis does compassion arise. "Okay, I'll listen now." We don't need to get to that point.

In truth our bodies are made of stardust. We are earth, water, wind, and fire; the elements of the body are the same as the elements of the earth. We are nature itself, manifest in these human forms. Symptoms are to be investigated, not suppressed. To live deeply within your body is to be juicy, fierce, and alive.

Over the course of a human life span, we each end up consuming enormous amounts of toxins. From the air we breathe, to the water we drink and the foods we consume, each of us is knowingly or unknowingly ingesting toxic material constantly. This is primarily due to the western pharmaceutical culture, drugs, GMO foods, and constant exposure to everyday products that are chemically based. Over time this accumulation takes a very heavy toll on our bodies. Our sophisticated immune systems become overworked and various forms of sickness and disease slowly manifest. Our bodies are alive, energetic systems that are ceaselessly responsive to our environment and what is being consumed within that environment. A complete detox of the body to remove the accumulation of toxic energy is also a key to eradicating all the seeds of disease, suffering, and illness.

Another aspect of the physical process is the removal of blockages within the body due to the physical traumas we have experienced throughout our lives. Examples of this include: physical abuse, sexual abuse, surgeries, assaults, accidents, our own birth process, and any other experiences when the body was hurt or injured. We experience these blockages as chronic pain, knots, muscle spasms, and other similar symptoms. These blockages create suffering in the body as well as in the mind. These experiences can range from mild to severe, but each experience can leave an energetic blockage that must be healed and removed in order for us to regain our optimal health and vitality.

Some people use meditation practice to try to escape the body. In some traditions, the body is considered evil, and spiritual practice is about cutting ourselves off. If we think our bodies are sinful and ugly, this is our confusion to work through. Still, some religious teachings encourage us to escape from the body and deny our feelings, as though the body were a burden. When you enter communities that hold these beliefs, you can feel the disconnection and lack of joy in the room. People seem frozen in a cold, stuck energy. They end up living in their heads, not their hearts. In fact, the body is a sacred vessel, a doorway to awakening. The heart lives deep in the body and the only way to access love is through your body.

One thing I've noticed is how easy it is to dissociate. You can't be both numb and fully alive at the same time. To be *in your body*, you have to be willing to *feel* the ten thousand joys and ten thousand

sorrows, and be present with them. When something is really painful, we might get numb and not feel much of anything. The body
goes through the motions, but we're not really there. Dissociation
is a coping mechanism, a defense that we use to shield ourselves
from the suffering of life. But over time it makes us feel cut off and
dead. Shutting down is not a long-term solution. We have to be
willing to walk through the fire and bring ourselves back to life.

There's wisdom in turning toward what we need to learn. Feel
your body and see if you can begin to access its wealth of knowledge. In life, pain will arise, and it can be challenging to sit still and
stay with it. Our shoulders, backs, and bellies carry much of the
burden. Feel into the pain to see if a storehouse of buried experience is offering to reveal itself. Sometimes a teacher can help you
discern what it is. If the body is releasing sorrow or tension and you
are capable of staying present with the experience, you might need
to sit through waves of fear and difficult memories. At times, life
reviews appear on the screen of your mind, and you process that.
You're accessing stored trauma, feeling the places in the body that
are holding these memories.

I've witnessed a lot of healing through meditation. People who
were on medications for pain management have told me their pain
was lessened by meditation practice. The mind gets quiet, and we
open to new states of awareness. Trust your body to lead the way.
Bring awareness to the pain, and allow the body to release what
it has been holding. Sitting quietly, you might feel rage or sorrow
rising from a deep well. If you are embodied and rooted in love,
powerful openings can take place. Pain comes, bringing emotions;
then the tension dissolves and ancient knots are loosened. Sometimes it's painful; sometimes it's blissful, and we take in these
beautiful energies.

The body is all alive 24/7 and it responds to love and compassion, especially through touch. When someone hugs us, oxytocin is

released by the pituitary glands in our brains, lowering our blood pressure. Babies who aren't held fail to thrive; their bodies don't develop. An article in *Life Magazine* details the first week in the lives of tiny premature twin babies, each in a separate incubator.[2] One was very ill and not expected to live. A nurse, who became attached to these twin girls, disobeyed the hospital rules and placed the babies in a single incubator. The babies were just a few days old, and the healthier of the two, the strong one, threw an arm over her little sister in an endearing embrace. After a while, the small baby's heart stabilized and her temperature rose to normal. The article was titled "The Rescuing Hug."

All bodies respond to love and care by opening up, and they respond to hatred and violence by shutting down. Thich Nhat Hanh said, "The Earth will be safe when we feel safe in ourselves," when we feel safe in our own bodies.[3] When you're feeling overwhelmed, practice mindfulness of the body and trust what is happening. If we abandon embodiment, we abandon our heart and the ability to connect.

## VIBRATIONAL LEVEL OF THE HUMAN SYSTEM

In essence everything is made up of energy, and over time we learn to cultivate it and balance it. "Chi" is a Taoist word that translates as "intrinsic life energy." Meditation works not only on the physical and mental levels but also very deeply on this life energy or vibrational level. In addition to having a human body we also have a light body or astral body that over time can become damaged. Negative things can get lodged in our energetic systems resulting in energetic imbalances. These imbalances often become the cause of our mental suffering and dis-ease with life. A traumatic experience of any kind leaves behind an energetic imprint that over time builds into a heavy residue on the vibrational level. We can experience this as an energetic tear or a strong sense of our energy being blocked or constricted in some part of the body. Through meditation practice we can heal and discover for ourselves the principles of natural balance. Being in harmony with nature and ourselves, we become the calmness and relaxation we seek.

Meditation retreats can be shamanic. In Shamanism and Buddhism, healing takes place at a vibrational level; energies are released. As the mind lets go, the body follows. With all the wars, refugee crises, police shootings, and other horrific events of our day, we have to keep coming back to our bodies. Stress is extremely toxic for us. Herbert Benson, MD, studied the effects of yoga, tai chi, deep breathing, and visualization on the body, and he discovered "the relaxation response," the quelling of pain and the inhibition of the stress hormones cortisol and adrenalin.[4] Dr. Benson saw that when people do these practices, their heart rates slow, blood pressure falls, digestion improves, and immune systems soar.

Sometimes our bodies know what's happening before we do. I'd been living in a house in Oakland that I loved, but it was in a rough neighborhood, and my body would shake whenever I was home. I knew I needed to move but I loved the house so much. My mind felt fine, but my body was trying to tell me something. So I got quiet and asked my body: What's up? What do I need to know? Soon I was shaking all night long and it wouldn't stop until I left home the next morning. As soon as I got back home, I would start shaking again. Eventually, I realized I needed to move. It didn't make sense to me, but I respected the information I was receiving from my body. Two days after I left, there was a terrible break-in, and I might have been hurt. If I hadn't listened to my body and only paid attention to my rational mind, I wouldn't have protected myself from harm.

Many of us have the power of feeling with our hearts. There's a certain attunement. We can feel our way intuitively. We feel when something is off, and we get a sense when things are going well. We need to tune in and listen to our intuition with respect. On the spiritual path, we learn to trust our body's natural wisdom. Our intuition or gut instincts are the body's way of alerting us to something important. Your body can begin to work with you. It's alive, and it's responsive to love and compassion. It wants to be free and happy just like everything else. By learning to live in your body, you begin to access this deeper wisdom. Our meditation practice helps us reconnect with our bodies, not just to heal trauma but to access the wisdom that is there. Body-based meditations and therapies can help us reconnect to our wisdom.

I've been practicing meditation for more than twenty years, and I still encounter traumas and blocked energy in my body. At first, they always feel like obstacles—some seem huge as boulders—but really they're all gifts, invitations to awaken and free myself. Patience is necessary, along with courage, equanimity, and self-care. I always learn from those experiences; I am still learning so much every day.

Awakening in your body is a powerful path and not always easy. Practice in a way that brings in compassion. If your body is suffering and you don't know what's happening, take time to give it your full attention. Dialogue with your body. Ask your body, "What is it you want me to know?" When you are hurting, ask what is at the root, and you'll get answers. Sit in meditation and feel your breathing and sensations. Do yoga, movement, walk, and dance whenever possible. Stay present, do your work, take care of your body and be mindful of what you put into it. Always try to bring a warm, motherly energy to your body. Be gentle, nourish yourself; be willing to feel. Your body is your sacred tree of life and it needs you.

We are not here to perfect ourselves, we are here to perfect our love.

—JACK KORNFIELD

## CHAPTER THIRTEEN

# LOVE IS THE ANSWER

THERE IS AN ANCIENT Amazonian and Mayan prophecy about the eagle and the condor. The eagle represents the masculine: the mind, action, technology, and structure. In North America, the eagle is heavily associated with the military, control, and dominance. The condor represents more of the feminine: compassion, Gaia, love, the community, and the heart. The condor is a magical creature in South America. The prophecy states that for five hundred years the eagle cultures will dominate the condor cultures until we land in a crisis. Then the condor will gain its strength once again. Then the condor will fly alongside the eagle, creating balance between the head and the heart. For us to attain wholeness, wisdom and love must work together. They are two sides of ourselves but they have been out of balance for a long time. It's time to focus on the heart once again.

Learning to love yourself is one of the hardest things you will ever do. I always say that love is the answer, and some people ask me, "The answer to what?" The answer to all life's questions. When I began to meditate, I would come home from a super-hard three-month retreat and my family would ask, "Did you have a nice vacation, Sweetie?" I'd say, "Are you kidding? It was brutal! I was purifying my mind." They'd look at me and didn't have a clue what I'd been through.

This is the Path of Purification. We scrub away the dirt and debris; its time for all of us to take the trash out. A great Burmese meditation master once told me that practicing meditation is like going to the beauty parlor for the inside. In many ways that is exactly what we are doing when we meditate, we are cleaning and beautifying our minds. This is purification. It's like putting the mind through a washing machine, scrubbing all the dirt, debris, and garbage out. Without purification, our minds become junkyards, littered with old Coke bottles, cigarette butts, graffiti, and trash. We get stuck in the mud and muck, and don't know how to get out. Meditation transforms garbage into compost, plants wholesome seeds, and helps us grow a beautiful garden within ourselves.

We all want to be free, happy, and to love ourselves; but wanting is not enough. When we are serious about freeing ourselves from the prisons of the mind, we need to begin *training* our own mind. We observe which intentions, thoughts, and actions create happiness and which ones bring about misery. We can wish for happiness until we're blue in the face, but if we act in ways that plant seeds of unhappiness, that is what we'll harvest.

Self-hatred is an epidemic in the West. It's the collective poison in the well water, and we all drink from it. It undermines all our best intentions. Starting at a young age, I saw it in myself—the self-judgment, the cruelty, the inner critic. We wake up with it, and it's our drumbeat all day long, commenting on everything, the constant negative monologue. We view ourselves with aversion. We hate our bodies and everything else about us. Self-hatred contaminates everything we do and worse it destroys our confidence and self esteem. We all have a self-destructive voice like this. The goal is to transform it. We have to. It's a lie. To hate ourselves is a form of complete insanity, and self-love is the answer and the cure. Rumi wrote,

> A pearl goes up on the auction block.
> No one bids.
> So the pearl buys itself.[1]

One night during my five-month retreat in Crestone, Colorado, I had a powerful experience. A beautiful, celestial, radiant angel visited me in a dream. She looked at me and asked, "Are you ready to let go of all your weapons?" I had suffered so much by this point in my retreat and I saw how the roots of my suffering were in self-hatred and anger. So I said yes immediately, and from the center of my chest—my heart—came all these weapons: semi-automatic rifles, pistols, knives, martial arts weapons, and medieval weapons like sticks with big metal bonkers on the end. Then a whole army started to come out, with tanks and military vehicles. I had a physical reaction, it was a deep sigh, and it went on and on for a very long time. There were ninjas and assassins of all types and little spinning weapons that maybe I'd seen in movies when I was young. This went on for at least half an hour.

Then I woke up shaking, with a feeling of being naked and scared. I curled up in the fetal position and felt alone and very vulnerable; and then I thought, "I've been disarmed." I felt that without my defenses—barbed wire, surveillance, alarm systems, codes, even alligators—I'd be annihilated. Then I remember feeling, "I don't actually need all these weapons anymore." I saw that, in fact, these weapons had been pointed at *me*. I'd thought they were about keeping others out, but it was an elaborate prison of the ego keeping me in. So I died to my confused perception and was reborn into reality. And without my defenses, I felt so vulnerable. Shortly after that event I laid down on the earth, like a snow angel and I realized, "There's power in self love, inner disarmament. I am disarming myself. I am learning how to love myself."

The poet Hafiz wrote, "Fear is the cheapest room in the house. I'd like to see you living in better conditions." We're terrified to open our hearts. What am I going to feel? What door am I walking through? These barriers are rooted in fear—fear of being abandoned, of feeling too much, of getting hurt, of annihilation. If I open, then what? We have so many defenses.

The practice of Metta is a very powerful and systematic way to develop genuine self-love. Metta is self-respect, being able to look in the mirror and say, "Thank you, beloved. I honor and respect you." It's not pride or ego. It's valuing our own spirit, the part of us that is noble and wise. Through the practice we learn to feed the good wolf. When you love yourself, loving others comes naturally. The Pali word *Metta* derives from the word that means "friendliness." It's often translated "loving kindness." Metta is wise love. It's more than warm feelings, ordinary affection, sentimental love, or the desire to possess. Metta is free from attachment. It's openhearted and generous. It doesn't exclude anyone and doesn't seek anything in return. It's the sun that shines on everyone. It doesn't choose "you, and you, and maybe you, but definitely not you." It's the radiant heart, open and inclusive. It's the authentic, unconditional acceptance that we all long for.

Our culture is obsessed with love, but, as with many things, we are confused so we look for it in all the wrong places. We want it, and failing to find it leads to pain and misunderstanding. We associate love primarily with romance—looking for love in order to feel complete. We think love is outside us and, to find it, we sacrifice a part of ourselves in our longing for acceptance. This is love with attachment. "I'll love you if you love me back. I'll love you if you will be who I want you to be." We want recognition and acknowledgment, and we look desperately for love from our peers, families, partners, and our communities, even our jobs. In our quest for love, we often sacrifice our own truth and authenticity and at the end of the day we never get what we truly want.

My parents knew very little about love. They weren't abusive, but they didn't know how to nurture their children in any significant way. They were abandoned so that is what they did to us. They themselves were children seeking love; so giving love was difficult for them. You can only give what you have and know. This has impacted my whole life. I grew up seeking attention everywhere. It wasn't until I learned about Metta that I realized that the love I needed I could give to myself. This was such a relief and over time I became stronger and stronger.

Many years ago I decided to do a six-week Metta retreat; I practiced loving kindness meditations nonstop. While walking, sitting, and eating, waking up and going to bed, I sent thoughts of loving kindness to those I care for, those I dislike, all beings, the whole cosmos, and myself. Suddenly I realized that the love I'd been looking for was this very love and that I am capable of generating it myself. I could turn loving kindness on like a bright light and radiate it outward, or inward. I didn't need anyone else to say, "I love you." I didn't need acknowledgment from the outside. All I needed was to generate the energy of Metta, and the love would shine brightly—and it was all generated from within. Realizing this, I began crying. I can feel love, acknowledgment, and recognition in *any* moment. I don't have to wait for others to love me. The great mystic and poet Rumi wrote that your task is not to seek for love, but merely to seek and find all the barriers within yourself that you have built against it.

We must learn how to practice loving ourselves. It's a step-by-step process. It's so profound and we're all just discovering how powerful this practice is. For me, I'm still learning, even after years and years.

Metta is the medicine that transforms anger, sorrow, and numbness. To begin, sit down in a quiet place, put your hand on your heart, and focus on self-care, compassion, and kindness. Visualize yourself sitting in front of you. Imagine that you are inhaling peace and exhaling kindness. Feel the love that surrounds you. Then recite, silently or aloud, phrases like, "May I be happy and peaceful. May I be safe and protected wherever I go. May I be healthy and strong in my body. May I live with ease and well-being." Offer yourself an inner bow, a visualized flower, or some kindness, honoring your practice, bowing to the highest part of yourself, the awakened being that lives in you.

The Metta practice is a form of radical purification that works to purify three distinct areas. The first is anger and hatred. Any time you declare to the universe that you are going to love yourself, look out! Everything that is not love will rise to the surface. Sometimes we sit and practice saying silently, "May I be happy. May I be peaceful," and a surge of hatred arises. You might think, "This isn't working." How is it possible that you're sending yourself love, and hatred comes back at you? The blocks to opening the heart are revealing themselves. Now you have something to work with. Anger and hatred, especially self-hatred, are to be expected when doing any heart practice. The confused mind is at war with itself. This is exactly what you're healing; don't give up!

The second thing Metta purifies and heals is sorrow. When I began practicing, I didn't experience much anger; that was too buried for me to access right away. But I did feel an intense sorrow. It was like meeting myself after being away for a long time, a reunion with a long-lost friend. When you're getting closer to something precious, your heart breaks open. The tears are part of the healing process, like a cleanse. We're removing walls and expanding the places that are the tightest. When we're willing to be open, our heart gets touched. When we see how precious we are and how harsh we've been, something inside us just breaks. It's like you blame someone for something and then find out he or she didn't do it. Then you're like, "Oh no!"—right? Then you're just full of remorse. The tears have the quality of homesickness; it's a purification we have to go through. For me, oceans of tears would just pour out and I would just stay present and keep doing it.

The third thing you'll encounter when you begin practicing Metta is numbness. You feel nothing. There's a block; you might feel an energetic block—tightness in your chest or a feeling of being stuck. Some meditators think, "I don't feel it. It's not working." Be patient. It happens one drop at a time. We've all been let down, betrayed, hurt, and abandoned. Healing a wound that has been sealed for decades won't happen in a thirty-minute meditation. The work is to soften those blocks, to open what has been closed for a long time. Through Metta practice, we begin to discover how big the block is. If you're not feeling anything, it's okay. Your body is shut down, and we work through that. Have faith in the practice. We just keep going and eventually we start to dismantle it. At times you will feel it and at other times you will feel nothing; it's all a part of the practice. You may want out, but stay with it. Numbness has to be met with the same loving, self-care with which we meet anything else. This is a powerful practice. You're learning to feel, embody, and open.

The practice of Metta can be truly healing because love is a refuge. A loving heart can make us feel safe. We can even learn to love our aches and pains, our tormenting thoughts, our rage, and our sorrow. We can hold these states with kindness. It might seem impossible at first. When I began practicing Metta, I would cry about the sadness I had experienced. But I kept practicing, and it was purification. Some people hate Metta practice in the beginning.

It feels fake. At first, I did too. I thought to myself, "May I be happy, may I be peaceful, blah, blah, blah." But I kept doing it, and something inside me, beneath the layers of my wounded skepticism, was able to let it in, and transformation began at a level deeper than my awareness. Something buried within us recognizes the intention to wish ourselves love. If we want to change, it's not going to happen from the outside. Others can't do it for us. We have to transform our own hearts. Loving yourself is something only you can do.

When you feel stable, send some of this energy to your family, friends, community, and loved ones, to your partner and coworkers. "May our communities be happy and peaceful. May our people be safe and protected. May all beings be healthy and strong." Send this energy out to your town or city, wishing everyone well. "May all beings everywhere live with joy, ease, and well-being. May all beings everywhere be happy and peaceful, safe and protected, healthy and strong, and may all of creation live with ease and joy." The body responds to love and compassion.

We each have our unique path to healing, uncovering levels of love and compassion as we are ready. It's like a labyrinth. You just keep going, discovering layers of your heart step by step. Anything that happens during the practice is acceptable. Whatever mind-state, whatever place you get caught, a trauma, a storyline that you can't get out of, it's all acceptable. This is what we're here to explore. Our minds are in a constant fight. To end this war, I recommend the practice of Metta. Love is the answer to all life's questions.

There is power, strength, and courage in love. All we have to do is keep opening our heart. The heart knows how to find its way home. In the end, Siddhartha defeated the powerful demon Mara by using love and compassion. On his night of enlightenment Mara attacked Siddhartha with a ferocious army of over 10,000 soldiers. Instead of responding in hatred, it's said that Siddhartha simply held up his hand, and all the bullets and arrows were transformed into flowers.

In his most challenging moment, what was Siddhartha's weapon of choice? It was love. Siddhartha recognized that the demon Mara was inside his own mind and he conquered him by invoking the power of love. We can train in that. We can awaken to that. There's no right or wrong, only understanding or not understanding the way things are. There's no sin, just unskillfulness. Instead of hatred, we sow love. Instead of doubt, we sow faith in ourselves. We plant seeds in the heart, cultivating the power of love.

The path to healing includes transforming all our demons. As we meditate, sitting quietly and walking slowly, we observe thousands and thousands of stories, images, fears, and desires. Anger, sadness, longing, and anxiety come and go. When we learn to meet these experiences with love and acceptance—loving what is—it's the essence of Metta. We meet each experience with love.

So do your practice, even if you don't enjoy it. Practice self-love, transform your heart, and forgive everyone who has ever done anything to harm you. Let go of anger and discover a more powerful force. Let love have you, it's who you are; and when it grows you become aligned with a power so bright it will shock you. You don't know how much time you have left on this planet. How do you want to spend your precious time?

Be patient with yourself. As the Dalai Lama said, "My religion is kindness."[2] Come back to the present moment over and over again. If we didn't grow up with these teachings, so it takes a while to train our minds, to allow this energy to seep into the fibers of our being so we can understand what it even means to be present, to be loving. Metta practice works if you plant the seeds, put in your time, and do it again and again. It might feel as though nothing's happening; and then suddenly you're in your own garden, everything is blooming, and there you are. The Buddha said that the greatest protection in all the world is love and kindness.[3]

"Love after Love" by Derek Walcott

The time will come
when, with elation
you will greet yourself arriving
at your own door, in your own mirror
and each will smile at the other's welcome,
and say, sit here. Eat.
You will love again the stranger who was your self.
Give wine. Give bread. Give back your heart
to itself, to the stranger who has loved you
all your life, whom you've ignored
for another, who knows you by heart.
Take down the love letters from the bookshelf,
the photographs, the desperate notes,
peel your own image from the mirror.
Sit. Feast on your life.[4]

Our goal is to create a beloved community and this will require a qualitative change in our souls as well as a quantitative change in our lives.

**—DR. MARTIN LUTHER KING JR.**

CHAPTER FOURTEEN

# A DREAM
# IS BORN

I'VE HEARD A LAKOTA PROPHECY, attributed to Crazy Horse, which says: I see a time of seven generations when all colors of mankind will gather under the sacred tree of life and the whole world will become one sacred circle again. We are the seventh generation. I feel blessed to be one of the founders of the East Bay Meditation Center (EBMC), now known as one of the most diverse and welcoming Dharma centers in the United States.

Creating an urban meditation center focused on serving diverse, disenfranchised communities, accessible, radically inclusive and relying solely on generosity-based economics was a vision a group of us shared, and through a beautiful, collective effort, this dream came true. In 2007, we opened our doors on a street corner in downtown Oakland, and we continue to grow and thrive today. My heart knew a place like this was desperately needed, so I dedicated myself to making this vision happen. It took a lot of years, hard work, and heaps of faith, but all things are possible through love and compassion. Harriet Tubman once said that every great dream begins with a dreamer; always remember, you have within you the strength, the patience, and the passion to reach for the stars to change the world.

The East Bay Meditation Center is a do-it-yourself, community-based organization. A collective effort supported by many loving people, volunteers, and a small, dedicated staff keep EBMC going. Our doors are always open. We have classes, workshops, and day-long retreats 365 days a year. Beautiful groups gather every day for meditation practice and classes on wisdom and compassion. The walls are purple, with rainbow flags hanging in the windows. But what makes it most real is the community. Together we've made EBMC a spiritual home, a true refuge for thousands of people. Our Thursday night Sangha has been meeting for ten years. These Thursday nights are my soul food. We welcome newcomers as well as those who keep coming back. It always feels like a warm embrace. We laugh together and sometimes we cry; like a family, we support one another through hard times. We practice opening the heart and learning to be in the present moment. All teachings are provided with an open hand and an open heart. And beyond all else we see the innate wisdom in diversity; it's something I have come to cherish above all else.

In the early days of my meditation journey, I traveled to retreat centers throughout the US. I loved the teachings and the practices, but I always felt like an outsider. Groups were almost a hundred percent white and consisted mostly of middle-aged people or seniors. All the teachers were white, mostly from upper middle class backgrounds. Consistently, I would walk into a room and be the youngest practitioner and the only person of color, and this would trigger a feeling in me that I was in a community I felt excluded from. The racism and pain I had experienced growing up would arise in me constantly during that time.

This lack of diversity was disheartening. I was unable to communicate my sorrow to the white Dharma teachers in a way they could understand. Some advised me to "be *with* my suffering," others advised me to "let it go," and a few just stared blankly. Without understanding my life experience, they weren't able to advise me. I appreciated their responses in principle—being with suffering and letting go are worthwhile practices, but compassion was telling me to look more deeply, that I wasn't truly getting the support I needed. I felt drawn to the teachings with my whole heart, but something was missing. Despite my passion and connection with the teachings, the pain in my heart persisted and I wondered if I'd be able to sustain this noble path while feeling so alone. I wanted to be part of an inclusive community that reflected the diversity of the world, and something in me was crying out for change.

After a while, I realized that if I wanted to be part of a beautiful, diverse Sangha, I'd need to help create it. We formed a small, dedicated group, and we made it happen. It felt like the medicine my heart had been needing, and sure enough, through the process of co-creating the East Bay Meditation Center, so much healing has happened. Gathering with people who look like me, I can allow in both the pain and the support of others who know the experience of racism, as well as sexism and homophobia. We now have a place for those who feel like outsiders, the voiceless who've never felt safe or truly at home in this world.

When we begin to practice meditation, our suffering and traumas begin to surface. The pain around racism, hatred, and discrimination goes deep, and to understand how it affects us takes understanding and compassion. As a woman of color, I understand the complexities all too well. When I was very young, my mother met a new man, and we moved from our tiny apartment in the 'hood in LA to a middle-class suburb in Northern California. My mother desperately wanted a new life, to become successful, and achieve the American dream, and she felt her new boyfriend was the ticket. The separation from the vibrant community of my African American father was, for me, a severing of identity, culture, language, and pride, not unlike the native children taken from their homes and sent to boarding schools. Overnight my mother changed, no longer cherishing diversity. All she wanted now was for my sister and me to assimilate with white suburban America.

In the name of progress and in a sad attempt to fit into the dominant culture and adopt its values, something in me was torn. My mother's intentions may have been noble—she wanted to give me the best education so I would have opportunities—but the price my spirit had to pay was high. I was enrolled in an elite, all-white elementary school an hour outside of San Francisco. The school was top-notch, and my classmates were very wealthy. I went from seeing all brown and black people to being the only person of color. My family and I never really fit in. We lived in rented homes and apartments and were always two or three months behind paying the rent. We never had money—I remember going with my mother to clean houses on the weekend to make ends meet. My mother lied about our addresses, our income, our status, everything was pretend. I didn't have expensive clothes like the other kids; all my clothes were from a thrift store in a rich neighborhood.

I kept trying to fit in, but a strong sense of shame was setting in. At one point I even wanted to get a nose job and blue contact lenses. My classmates teased me about my hair and my brown legs, and every so often I was called a nigger. The worst racism was when I went to play at my friends' homes; some parents didn't want me around their children. The teachers were impatient and critical with me. I always got yelled at, and at one private school I was called into the principal's office where he hit me repeatedly with a large ruler for no apparent reason. At the same school I was forced to stand facing a brick wall. I stood for so long that my legs fell asleep, and I collapsed crying. I did receive an excellent education, but the impact on my heart was deadly. I spent those years feeling deeply depressed and, although no one knew, suicidal.

At the age of ten I was ready to end it all. I went on a weeklong camping trip with my fourth-grade class. I was very depressed and didn't want to go, but my mother forced me anyway. While we were out on a nature hike, one of the guides pointed to a plant with small, red berries and told us to be cautious because the berries were extremely poisonous and would cause rapid death. Soon after the hike, I went in search of the plant, and when I found it, I picked a handful of berries and came back to the dormitory to prepare myself. I wanted to pray before eating them.

As fate would have it, a sweet girl from another class came over to talk to me at that exact moment. She had a face like a fairy and a huge smile that comforted me. She spoke in this squeaky voice, and before long we were both laughing. She invited me outside, and then I realized that my hand was still clutching the berries. My palms were sweaty and it was becoming a mess, so I walked over to a tree and, with a long sigh, I let them go. My fairy friend stayed by my side the entire week, cheering me on and making me laugh. At the end of the week, we said our goodbyes and I never saw her again. I have no idea what prompted her to leave her class and join me, but I can only feel grateful. She arrived at the moment I needed a friend the most. The power of her angelic compassion still leaves me speechless with tears on my cheeks.

To make matters even more confusing, my mother had difficulty accepting that her children were half-black. At Christmas, we got white dolls and on our birthdays we got cards with little white children on them. My mother didn't acknowledge that I was African American until I was in my twenties. The distance between us grew every day.

By the time I was thirteen, my mother and I were arguing constantly. On the surface we struggled about the same things as moms and daughters everywhere. But more deeply, we were always fighting about race, culture, and identity. I longed for the community I'd left behind and lost all interest in fitting into the world she was a part of. Finally, I refused to go to the school she'd chosen and began to make new friends. My mother had changed so much. She'd once been a free spirit, but now she was conservative and didn't seem to have any sensitivity to what I was feeling. She made fun of the way I talked and couldn't understand why I wanted to be around "poor people," as she called my new friends. The funny thing was that we were the poor ones, living in a tiny apartment, barely getting by. Everything felt completely fake.

When I was fifteen, I decided to reclaim my life. I could no longer live with my mother and her abusive boyfriend. Separation from my African American self had been too painful for too long. Pride in being a brown woman invigorated me, and after a long separation from half of myself and communities of color, I moved back to Los Angeles to relearn how to be at home in my own skin. I had to rediscover who I was, so I could reclaim what had been lost. I felt sad leaving, but I knew I had to find my own path in life. I never lived with my mother after that; I was on my own.

To discover who I am, I went through the depths of hell. But it was all very important, and through it all, my interest in self-knowledge was unshakeable. As a teenager, I began studying psychology in order to treat my own depression. I read everything I could get my hands on to try to understand my mind. At twenty-three, I left Los Angeles and moved back to Oakland for good.

Issues of race, class, gender, and discrimination were not addressed at any of the meditation centers I encountered. No one ever talked about racism or diversity *ever*. It was a facet of the diamond left unpolished. I needed a practice that looked at everyone equally, that valued everyone's Buddha nature *and* their life experiences. Only then could my inner and outer worlds transform together, addressing the oppression and self-hatred that arise from ignorance based on scapegoating and projection.

Creating a loving, inclusive community has been a healing process for me and not always easy. We had to do things differently. I had to adjust and grow; I couldn't stay the same. The world we live in is changing. Values are changing, and an inclusive Dharma is needed for a global community that is colorful and diverse. On an absolute level, who we are doesn't matter. But on the level of the heart, race, gender, and sexual orientation matter, and discrimination takes its toll. As I awoke to this pain in my heart, the need to create something new to heal my beloved community and myself got stronger and stronger.

What I've discovered is that diversity is a radical form of inclusivity. In diverse communities, we grow more, because we have to consider the needs of others. We all have internal hierarchies, lines identifying who we let in and who we don't. Can we allow more and more people into our hearts? Diversity challenges these preferences and opinions and exposes our biases. As spiritual practitioners, we want to see our delusions so we can overcome them. One powerful delusion is that some of us are more valuable than others, that some are entitled to privileges that others are denied. Many well-meaning people are unaware of their biases. Our work is to shine light where there is darkness, not to perpetuate lies, even if it's done unconsciously. My sadness became a river of compassion, and I was ready to act.

We envisioned EBMC as a place for communities of color, LGBTQ, and the many people who often feel left out and unwanted. I thought, "I'm an open person," and then people came with chemical sensitivities and asked, "What about us?" Then people came and asked "Could we have a Spanish language group?" And I started to think, "I'm not sure we can fit everybody in." Then someone asked, "Could there be a group for trans people?" I started to feel the barriers to my love. "I only can go so far." But then I felt my heart expanding. "Yes, we can include all of you." Diversity forced my heart to open more than I realized was possible. All these people were coming with different needs, "We have this and that special need, and we need EBMC to be accessible, so Spring, can you change this?" I would encounter yet another resistance in myself, and then I would melt it. "What do you need?" That would open my heart even more, and now I see that opening to others' needs is a teaching, a tremendous gift—not as a place of conflict but as a place of learning and growth. Every new group needed us to change something so they could have a home at our center, and I got to see how I was clinging. It was painful, and liberating. "What about the person cleaning bathrooms in a hotel? How can I let them in my heart?" When we say we love all beings, what are we saying? When we practice these teachings, do we mean *all beings*, or the clique we have coffee with who are pretty much the same as us? Opening to diversity is a powerful teaching—not just as a noble ideal, but actually learning what it is to love all beings.

There's something profound about widening your circle. What you learn from different people is a mirror. Einstein said, "Our task must be to free ourselves by widening our circle of compassion to embrace all living creatures and the whole of nature and its beauty."[1] The only way to do that is to engage. Every person I look at is a reflection of my own mind. What am I resisting now? What am I pushing away? What do I not want to look at? What do I want to close off to? Every time I open the door, I grow.

Diversity was also a challenge for the Buddha. In ancient India, and in present-day India, there was a deeply ingrained caste system. But within his monastic community, the Buddha treated all as equal. His whole diverse community was expected to live together in harmony. Those considered "untouchable" by society sat alongside kings and princes. It was a bold move, and he gave many teachings on equality.

It is said that a relative of the Buddha, someone accustomed to palace life, asked to join the monastic community. The Buddha told him, "I'm happy to ordain you, cousin. Show up at such-and-such a time and bring your robes." All the monks wore the same type of robes, but his cousin came to his ordination with a fancy silk garment. "No, cousin. Here you are the same as every other person." The Buddha also ordained women, which was extremely controversial at the time.

To heal fully, we must heal the places of separation within our hearts. We can use our own suffering to create a lifeline to help others. I believe that I experienced the suffering I did so that I could understand the challenges of both sides. Walking in different worlds is my way, coming in and out of communities, reweaving myself, shape shifting to meet the needs of each. It was part of my trial by fire to practice in non-diverse communities. The suffering that arose became a gift. Everything that hurts us can be transformed in the fire of compassion to create something new to alleviate suffering, not just for ourselves but for the benefit of all beings. We are moved to dedicate ourselves to something bigger. My gifts come from the places I'm the most wounded, and my joy comes from alleviating the suffering I feel in my own heart.

I travel all over the world teaching retreats and workshops and visiting communities. In my heart, the East Bay Meditation Center is my true spiritual home. Thank you, beautiful community, for joining me on this amazing journey! There isn't enough darkness in all the world to snuff out the light of one little candle. We are that little candle and we will continue to shine brightly no matter how dark it gets. *AHO!* [2]

Rest in natural great peace this exhausted mind,
Beaten helplessly by karma and neurotic thoughts,
Like the relentless fury of the pounding waves
In the infinite ocean of samsara.
Rest in natural great peace.

**—NYOSHUL KHEN RINPOCHE**

## CHAPTER FIFTEEN

# ISLANDS OF PEACE

ON NOVEMBER 11, 2016, just a couple of days after the election of Donald Trump as the president of the United States, I was scheduled to teach in downtown Oakland for three days in a row. That night, I entered the East Bay Meditation Center to teach at the people of color community night, and there were two hundred people inside, a very full house. Our Sangha is usually around one hundred people, so it was a very full class. During the yoga class that had just ended, they had done a breathing practice called "breath of fire" and they set off all the fire alarms. The sorrow, fear, and rage in the room was palpable.

As I sat down and took a deep breath, I looked around—a rainbow of colors: people of all shades of brown skin, Native Americans and people whose ancestors had come, or been brought, to the US from Africa, Central and South America, the Middle East, and Asia.

We began with a silent meditation, and during the meditation, a large riot began to erupt a block away. Helicopters were flying overhead and police were shouting at protesters loudly on bull-horns. A volunteer approached me quietly during the meditation to ask if she could close the windows. Tear gas was beginning to slowly seep in. As I rang a large Tibetan bell to end the meditation, it was a surreal moment, one that none of us will ever forget. We were practicing meditation in the middle of a growing riot out-side, and we all had to deal with the riot that was exploding inside each of us.

During the next three days, I sat in circles with nearly five hun-dred people, all seeking answers, understanding, and a place to express the rawness of their emotions, but mostly to find comfort in being together. In the uncertainty of the moment, they wisely sought refuge in their spiritual community.

I often get stomachaches watching the news—all the wars, sense-less killings, racism, environmental destruction, and global trage-dies. This Earth is my home, a sacred altar, and it feels on the brink of collapse. When we look around, the whole project of life on Earth can feel hopeless and overwhelming. We hold this tension in our bodies and our hearts. Where can we go when things are this dif-ficult? What is a true place of refuge in the midst of so much over-whelming sorrow and uncertainty?

In the Buddhist tradition, humanity is sometimes described as being lost in a vast ocean. I always imagine all seven billion of us, dog paddling and flailing around desperately, looking for securi-ty, some safe place to stand. This is the ocean of samsara, the end-less cycle of our collective confusion. We all long for happiness, yet we unconsciously do the very things that lead to unhappiness. We drown over and over. In the midst of all the chaos, is there a place where we can find solid ground?

As we slow down and become present, we begin to see an island in the distance. We swim there and find a dry, sunny beach with a coconut tree we can sit beneath. We've found a place we're safe, a refuge from the pounding ocean. As we survey the ocean from our new perspective, we see millions of others flailing desperately, not yet able to see the island. We shout out to them, but they don't hear us. They're not ready yet. We look around at our new island home and see we are not alone. Others have taken refuge here as well.

We're living in a house of cards: all life is fragile, and we don't know what the future will bring. This is the nature of reality. It's always fluctuating; one day it's this, the next day it's that. There are multiple causes to everything that happens and an intelligence that governs everything lawfully. As soon as something arises, it begins to dissolve. Without steadiness, it can feel terrifying. The Buddha taught, "Live in joy and love, even among those who hate. Live in joy and health, even among the afflicted. Live in joy and peace, even among the troubled. Look within, be still, free from fear and attachment. Know the sweet joy of the Way."[1]

The Buddha advised us that the "way" is to *take refuge* during life's storms in order for us to find our island of peace amidst the pounding waves. There is an "inner" refuge and an "outer" refuge that we discover when everything else around us starts falling apart. The word *refuge* has several meanings such as sanctuary, shelter, protection, and haven, but ultimately the best translation is "a place of safety." There are three aspects to this teaching of refuge, three places of refuge we can rely on. They're known as the Three Jewels or the Three Gems in Buddhism: Buddha, the quality of wisdom in every human being; Dharma, the truth; and Sangha, the beloved community that surrounds the practitioner.

When we encounter difficulties in life, only a small handful of people know how to respond wisely. These individuals are able to stay upright and steady, even through the toughest storms, fires, and raging waters. The majority of us, though, struggle big-time. We're paddling our boats in the ocean of samsara and capsizing every ten minutes. Out of confusion, people act with greed, hatred, and delusion, and it leads them to harm others. We may take refuge in drugs, alcohol, sex, relationships, consumerism, hatred, workaholism, denial—the list goes on and on. We keep looking for solid ground but don't know where to find it.

The Buddha taught that there are three reliable islands of refuge that can provide us with an indestructible base, a powerful shelter that can withstand any storm. This unshakeable ground becomes the basis for wise action that's in alignment with our deepest intention and our heart's motivation. To navigate skillfully, we need a map, trustworthy directions, and faith in the Three Jewels.

## FIRST REFUGE: YOUR INNER BUDDHA

When we take refuge in our inner Buddha, it's not someone or something outside of ourselves. It's not any kind of outer god figure that we worship. "Buddha" is a state of consciousness, a state of being; it means, "awakened one." We access this part of our minds by living more and more in the present moment. We awaken to it by the practices that we do. Buddha nature can be described as our basic sanity, our own innate wisdom. What we learn to trust and take refuge in is that eternal wisdom which is within each of us. It can never be damaged or destroyed, it can only be temporarily hidden from view. We lose sight of it within ourselves, but it's always there; it's the jewel in the heart of the lotus flower. Our job now is to unveil it more and more. Through meditation practice, we clean the muck off the jewel. There is not a truer statement than "we are the ones we have been waiting for." We must begin to believe in ourselves.

*Buddha nature,* the capacity to awaken to our true nature, is at the core of every human being. We are hardwired to wake up and realize the truth of who we are. Buddha nature is in our cells, our genes, and our DNA. We are all born with the seed of Buddha nature, the ability to awaken to our truest essence of clarity, radiance, compassion, and wisdom. You may think some people are more worthy, based on ethnicity, gender, family lineage, sexual orientation, education, political or economic power. This, my friends, is a *big lie*. Everyone—and I mean everyone—has the eternal seed of awakening planted deeply in their own heart.

To develop a fierce heart, we must never forget our essence of Buddha nature. This state of complete freedom can be called self-realization, Christ consciousness, or by many other names. Whatever we call it, wherever we are, whatever we have been through, this seed inside of us has the potential to awaken. We just need to water it, nurture it, and help it grow.

While growing up, there was so much negative programming in my mind. We've all been brainwashed this way: I'm worthless. I'm a black woman, and so I'm on the low end of the totem pole. We operate as if we're flawed at the core, we feel ashamed of who we are, so we spend our lives hiding under the covers. At our core is something beautiful, wise, and whole. Watching people at the conclusion of retreats, I see their radiance. They're overflowing with joy and compassion. *This* is really who they are. Don't be fooled by the lies.

The year I was writing this book, there were so many videotaped police shootings of African American men. Witnessing the phenomenon of state sanctioned murder again and again was devastating, and that's one of the many reasons it's vital for people of color to see and celebrate our own radiance. No one can give you your power back; only you can do that. If someone says, "I love you, you're beautiful as you are, I see your light," you won't believe it unless you feel it in your soul. Others can encourage you, but they can't uncover the truth of who you are. According to the Buddha, at our core is this incredible beauty, wisdom, and compassion, and the more we practice, the clearer it gets and the more we recognize it.

Ultimately, it doesn't matter what people on the outside say or do. It's an internal switch we turn on or off. South African activist Steve Biko used to say that even though the lie, the outer conditions, are compelling, only our own mind can oppress us. Don't mistake the muck for your true nature. It doesn't matter how many people say the opposite, your true nature is luminous. Period. We have to reframe how we view ourselves. This is what it means to take refuge in the Buddha. If we can bring this teaching into every community, into one group after another, there will be a shift in consciousness. When you feel lost, go inside yourself and feel your own heart. Our practice is to remind ourselves who we are, over and over, until we never forget. When my sister and I were younger, any time something would go wrong or we would start freaking out about something, we would high-five each other and say, "It's all Buddha baby," then laugh. It was a reminder to come back to the present, to come back to our hearts.

In June 2011, I had the privilege of being present for the Dalai Lama's teaching ceremony called the Kalachakra for World Peace, a beautiful, elaborate Tibetan ritual. The monks built a huge sand mandala of the universe, and for ten days we blessed it as a way to elevate consciousness for world peace. Twenty-five thousand of us were in the Verizon Center in Washington D.C., listening to the Dalai Lama give a variety of talks and teachings. One day he stopped mid-sentence and said, "I hope you think enlightenment is possible," adding, "You have to believe that. If you don't really believe in awakening, if you don't really believe in Buddha, you'll never get there. You won't be able to set your compass there if you don't really believe that this is possible for every human being. You must understand this is true!" He was fired up. "You have to believe that."

It touched me. I was thinking of the refuge, the island, and setting my compass to that, aligning myself with that. I was inspired. Somewhere in me I questioned whether enlightenment is possible.

I'd been through so many traumas. Maybe I just want to feel a little better. If I could suffer a little less, I'd be good. Having modest expectations is okay too, but then we don't reap the real reward. We feel a little better, but we don't have liberating insight. There has to be some kind of alignment, some belief in enlightenment as a possibility, that each individual has the capacity to awaken their own heart and mind.

## SECOND REFUGE: THE DHARMA OF TRUTH

The Buddha was a physician, healer, priest, and shaman whose specialty was the mind. He examined thoughts, perceptions, and emotions and, based on what he saw, he offered diagnoses and treatment plans. For weeks after his awakening under the Bodhi tree, he reflected on his new insight and how to share it effectively. A clear formulation began to develop in his mind, a teaching that could help others to free their minds as he had freed his. Out of this deep, heartfelt wisdom and compassion, he went forth to share his understanding with others.

When the Buddha began his forty-five-year ministry, he called his teachings the Way to end suffering. The Yellow Brick Road is open, and it leads to the Emerald City of peace.

There's a parable that illustrates the Buddha's insight.[2] There is an enchanted city where everyone lives happily together in peace. There is no hunger, suffering, or discontent; it's a place of joy, abundance, and unconditional love. An ancient path leads directly to the city, but over time the path falls into disrepair and becomes harder and harder to find. Eventually it gets covered over and is in danger of being lost and forgotten. Siddhartha, with great love and perseverance, rediscovers the path to this Ancient city. He didn't invent the path. It's an ancient path; it's been there since the beginning of time. Siddhartha painstakingly cleared the debris, moved the boulders, and cut back the branches. Later he put up road signs and began directing people to follow this ancient path, so they could once again enter the city of Nirvana.

The Dharma is the treatment plan; it's the spiritual path that's based on ethics, mind training, and wisdom. Out of our awareness of cause and effect, we start planting seeds of compassion, wisdom, love, devotion, and service, and moving away from planting other seeds. And through purification, we pull out some of the unwholesome roots. The more we pay attention, the more we see how happiness is created and how suffering is created. We understand the Four Noble Truths and that becomes our view. We move toward wholesome, skillful actions, because it is less painful. We don't do it because we *should,* we do it because we've learned. When we *choose* to be free and are willing to do the work to get there, healing is possible. We practice mindful breathing, mindful walking, and compassion, and reality can reveal itself.

When we take refuge in the Dharma, we cherish the teachings. We have thousands of maps left behind by great beings in every tradition, from every region of the Earth. These mapmakers of the soul have left us timeless instructions, teachings, music, and poetry. All of it is the Dharma. "Here's the way. Follow this path, your fierce heart knows the way home." The Buddha didn't invent the Dharma. He just cleared the ancient path from what was obscuring it. If you have a trail and don't clear it once a year, you lose it, and no one can find it. Someone has to come and clear it and put trail markers on it. The Buddha and the wise ones of every tradition have done that for us. And we have many living examples of teachers in our day who help us walk it. In this way, we take refuge in the Dharma, it's alive, the timeless truth of the way things are, the vibrancy of the present moment.

## THE THIRD REFUGE: THE AWAKENED COMMUNITY

The word *Sangha* is translated as the beloved community. It is a place of nonjudgmental acceptance, a place where it's safe to be honest and open and free. In the Sangha, life's challenges can be faced in a supportive, loving environment. Friendships and community are important aspects of the practice. We're there for each other on many levels. When you have a community of beautiful people in your life, you know you can count on them and that is both supportive and healing. Many of us grew up in environments where we couldn't count on the people around us. In a good Sangha, we can open our hearts in ways we haven't before. Sangha means the beloved, sacred, and holy community.

In the Sangha, people come together to practice freedom together. It's rare when a group of people is in total alignment. The Sangha includes communities all over the world where people are practicing. Right now, someone is ringing a bell, getting ready to practice meditation. It's all part of the sacred Sangha. The Sangha also includes beings who have died and left behind teachings that point the way. All that and more, together, make a powerful refuge. Where do you go when you need help? To the Sangha, your spiritual community.

Thich Nhat Hanh has said that the future Buddha will be a community. We take refuge in all the beings who have discovered the path, walked the path, and gone all the way to the end. We take refuge in the Sangha of all the people along the way, our comrades and friends, everyone we encounter in any community of people. When we feel alone, not knowing what to do, we can remember the Sangha, the many friends and groups along the path. As Margaret Meade wrote, "Never doubt that a small group of thoughtful, committed citizens can change the world. Indeed, it's the only thing that ever has."[3]

Look around and see who is with you all the time. Are they people who think the way you do, who support your vision, who value wisdom? Or are you around people whose values are less elevated? When you're being pulled down, it's easy to forget yourself and what you care about most. When you're around certain people, all that goes out of the window and you act in ways that don't satisfy yourself deeply. You wake up the next day and you're like, "What was that about? I was doing better. I want to purify that." I want a Sangha to be my wisdom council, a community that reflects my values, where I cherish my friends who are with me on the path.

I cherish my wise and beautiful friends. Many are teachers and friends I met at retreats. We get together and we cry in gratitude. I'm elevated by their presence in my life. They help me remember. When I forget, there's someone to go to, someone to remind me what we're doing, to offer counsel on how to respond to this or that situation.

Your Sangha becomes your mirror. Like-minded people like spending time together. If you're a mathematics genius, you hang out with math professors and others who share your passion. In spiritual communities where people are trying to wake up, they live with others on the path—in monasteries, residential centers, and communities where folks practice together and support each other. We all contribute and help each other grow.

One day the Buddha's cousin Ananda asked the Buddha, "Noble one, I hear that friends are half of the holy life." And the Buddha replied, "No, Ananda, friends are *the whole* of the holy life."[4] Everyone in the community is part of your Sangha. At the retreat center, this includes the people chopping vegetables for your meals, those cleaning the bathrooms, sweeping the floors, teaching, doing the admin, and organizing. In the Sangha, we support each other in our awakenings. We give and receive advice, inspiration, and support.

If we stand together, with compassion, there is no more important response to the obstacles we all face. At a fundraiser, Jack Kornfield led a forgiveness practice. A thousand people were there, and they soaked in the teachings. It was beautiful to see people standing with all those who are often discarded. That is the fierce heart. Our willingness to stand in our teachings is critical right now. Most important is taking refuge in the Sangha. Our communities are rising. We see it everywhere. Young people are moving into groups, living together, farming together, living off the grid, sharing, beginning anew; they are creating a new society. Your Sangha is a refuge. You need your Sangha no matter what stage of life you are in.

And your Sangha needs you. When we're born we need community, when we're young we need community, as we age we need our community. It's an illusion to think that we can do it alone. The Buddha lived his whole life in community. He did not live alone on a mountaintop. The teachings in the great texts are filled with stories of community, of how they learn together. How can we grow and nurture community? In difficult times, where do you go? You reach out to a friend. You look for support.

I feel blessed to have so many wise people in my life. When I need guidance, I call someone and get really good wisdom. Each friend, each elder has his or her vantage point. "Remember awareness," they say. "Remember the heart. Remember emptiness. Remember impermanence. Be with metta." The Buddha said the Sangha is the most precious gem.

Dr. Martin Luther King wrote, "Love is creative and redemptive. Love builds up and unites.... The aftermath of love is reconciliation and creation of the beloved community."[5] A few days after the fatal shooting of twenty children at Sandy Hook Elementary School, I led a daylong meditation retreat at our center in downtown Oakland. The theme was "Opening the Heart and Living with a Wise Heart." What had happened at that school in Connecticut was in the air; everyone was talking about it. The sadness touched a nerve in all of us. On TV, I saw that even the President was crying. The Sangha is pivotal to this beloved community that's evolving.

As our world gets more fractured, we have to learn to work together. The age of the isolated individual, the go-it-alone pioneer, is over. How many of us can work together to solve these problems? How many of us can create new, clean food sources? How many of us can live together? How many of us can grow together? Gandhi said, "Let us work together for unity and love."[6] It's so simple. In the midst of all the violence in the world, there is so much kindness too. We have to hold both, the joys and the sorrows. At the end of the day, compassion will save us.

The heart of a Buddha is a heart filled with compassion. Wherever I go, people ask, "How can I help? Do you need anything?" There is so much kindness all around us, and as you open to this truth you will find the Three Refuges. When things fall apart, we take refuge in the Three Jewels and these become our islands of peace.

The broken world waits in darkness for the light that is you.

—L. R. KNOST

## CHAPTER SIXTEEN

# FOR THE BENEFIT OF ALL BEINGS

EVERY GREAT MYTH about the hero's journey entails a cycle of departure, transformation, and return. At the end of the story, the hero or heroine returns to their community to bring back the newfound knowledge, wisdom, and medicine they have bravely acquired. Most significant of all, they return transformed and ready to begin a life of service. We see versions of this returning hero archetype in works of art, in *Star Wars, Avatar,* and in the lives of great women and men all over the world. Archetypes are the patterns, images, and symbols that appear in dreams, myths, and fairy tales. They represent the instincts shared by all humans toward compassion and the many other qualities that are collective, ancestral, and bigger than any individual. The great myths are our stories. As we grow in the practice, we start to move in the direction of heroism. Ultimately, the hero surrenders their life to something much bigger than themselves.

Siddhartha spent six long years in the forest trying to undo the tangle of his mind. The climax of his struggle was an epic show-down with Mara, the chief demon, the ultimate personification of greed, hatred, and delusion. As Siddhartha sat under the bodhi tree, Mara's armies ferociously attacked him over and over. In the end, he was able to conquer them all and discover the great truth he had sought for so long. After his six years in the forest and his encounter with Mara under the bodhi tree, Siddhartha, now a Buddha, returned to his family's home and community. He had discovered spiritual truths that he wanted to share, and he offered teachings to his former wife and his father, and then he passed these teachings on to his young son. All of them understood the depth of his message and they became devoted followers. Shortly thereafter, the Buddha left his home a second time, this time as a great spiritual teacher. He would go on to teach for forty-five years, setting in motion one of the biggest spiritual movements on the planet, which has lasted for more than 2,500 years and continues to grow in the present day.

We all go through hardships, wherever our journey takes us. Our lives may look different, but we—and all heroes and heroines—face difficulties and tests along the road of trials. In every mythical story, there's a moment when the hero feels unprepared to go forward, and yet he or she has to find the strength to keep going. We all reach a point when we believe, "I can't overcome this problem," then we do and we learn how to meet the challenges as they come. We encounter those places in ourselves that we thought we could never be open to; but now, even when we feel overwhelmed, we stay present with them and we grow.

When we can't see clearly ahead and we don't know whether to turn left or right, we go forward anyway. An aspect of faith is trusting that life is happening for us and not to us. When we experience this support, our energy is freed up and we find the courage of a warrior. There are moments in life when we genuinely don't know what to do. Yet we have to move in some direction. Freedom requires us to move toward our goal. If we have that faith, we'll see that everything is happening for a reason and on time, and we can move with a certain grace and trust, even if it's risky. We can't always play it safe; sometimes we have to seize the moment and act boldly. This is part of the hero's journey, finding our strength and learning to trust our gut instincts.

We don't always know what's going to happen, and there are always demons, trials, and struggles. And just as we're about to get out of the prison of our own creation, the most intense demon of all stands before us. When the Buddha conquered Mara, the greatest demon, he placed his hand on the Earth, roared like a lion, and declared his right to be free. That is what we all have to do at times. We declare our power and our right to be free. We do this while trusting in the higher intelligence that is guiding our lives. The more we transform ourselves, the more tests we face; it's part of the journey, it's all part of the bigger story in which our lives are playing out. Every challenge is meant to wake us up so that we can learn and become able to benefit others when the time is right. One human being who opens their heart can inspire many others. Never underestimate the power of love and compassion.

A Bodhisattva is someone determined to free others from the harmful effects of greed, hatred, and delusion. It's a core theme in the Mahayana Buddhist tradition and it's said that Prince Siddhartha had been a practicing Bodhisattva for countless lifetimes. Taking Bodhisattva vows is a commitment, and it is one I have taken many times with some great masters. Bodhisattva means "awakening being" or "one who understands the nature of things." The word *bodhisattva* is sometimes translated as "enlightened hero," one whose every action is for the benefit of others.

Bodhisattvas often make vows to walk into hell for a heavenly cause. They commit themselves fully to a life of service. I feel that true Bodhisattvas are the descendants of awakened beings. They are part of a living web of celestial beings, *devas* (gods), and Dharma protectors who support their heroic intentions to serve others. They use the challenges and sufferings of life in order to wake up. With each experience, they ask, "What can I learn? How can I grow?" Bodhisattvas are moved into action by soul force and fierce compassion. They don't shy away from difficulties; they relish them.

Bodhisattvas appear in many forms, including environmentalists, teachers, activists, artists, musicians, and everyday people who work to alleviate the suffering of others because they care. The movement is growing. Motivated by compassion and understanding interconnectedness, bodhisattvas work day and night to step off the wheel of suffering and become a light in the darkness. If just a few people wake up, their awakening will affect the whole world.

Every morning, the Dalai Lama recites a prayer called the "Bodhisattva Prayer for Humanity," composed by Shantideva, an eighth-century Indian Buddhist sage:

**Bodhisattva Prayer for Humanity**[1]
May I be a guard for those who need protection
A guide for those on the path
A boat, a raft, a bridge for those who wish to
cross the flood
May I be a lamp in the darkness
A resting place for the weary
A healing medicine for all who are sick
A vase of plenty, a tree of miracles
And for the boundless multitudes of living beings
May I bring sustenance and awakening
Enduring like the earth and sky
Until all beings are freed from sorrow
And all are awakened.

I would never have been able to keep going in the face of so many difficulties if it had been just me that mattered. I had to have a bigger motivation than that. While on retreats I would often suffer, but when I would think about the state of the world or my community at home, an inner strength would come over me. I would think about the children in the world who are suffering and the women struggling to feed their families. This power would give me the courage to keep going so that one day, I might be able to help alleviate some of the suffering in this world. "For the benefit of all beings" is not just a recitation practice. For me, it's my life; it gives me wings and the motivation to keep going. My joy comes from this.

Last year, Jack Kornfield and Alice Walker did a benefit for the East Bay Meditation Center called "Fierce Love in Times of Conflict." I asked Alice, "How do we love people who hate us?" This was a few days after the mass shooting at an LGBTQ nightclub in Orlando, Florida, and many in our community were hurting. Her answer was immediate, "We have to understand that people are programmed, they are taught to hate." It's the programming and conditioning that is so destructive; it's a form of sickness. She told stories about doing voter registration in the late sixties in Mississippi. She talked about how prepared people were to die. Yet they were happy. They had parties and would tell each other, "If we die like this, let it be so." The KKK left hate mail in their mailboxes, but they just ignored it. They were determined. They felt so committed to the rightness of what they were doing and there was such love between them, that they were not afraid of dying. People are feeling the need to stand with others now, even at the risk of their own lives. We don't need brute force when we have soul force. Soul force is the power of truth in action and it's fierce.

Interconnectedness is a fundamental teaching in Buddhism, and it's a part of what motivates us to act compassionately. It's a worldview that sees oneness in all things. Separation exists only on the level of appearances. The deluded mind sees separation and says, "You are different." You speak a different language or your skin is darker or there's something else that makes you seem separate. But there is so much beneath that. Beneath the surface, everything is interwoven. Ecologist and social justice activist Joanna Macy sums it up this way: "Our lives are as inextricably interwoven as the nerve cells in the mind of a Great Being."[2]

While incarcerated in Birmingham, Alabama, Dr. Martin Luther King Jr. wrote, "All life is interrelated. All men are caught in an inescapable network of mutuality, tied in a single garment of destiny. Whatever affects one directly affects all indirectly. I can never be what I ought to be until you are what you ought to be, and you can never be what you ought to be until I am what I ought to be. This is the interrelated structure of reality."[3] All things are interconnected. They are of a single underlying reality. Deep within, there is no separation. We are all a part of this universal oneness.

To do the work he did, Dr. King had to see this clearly. Freedom, in his mind, wasn't just for one group. It was for everyone—those filled with hatred and those who were being oppressed. He understood that for him to be free, everyone needs to be free. He couldn't have done all that he did unless he realized it wasn't just about him. It was about something bigger than any one of us. He vowed to free the oppressed and the oppressors from the effects of greed, hatred, and delusion. This is the power of love.

Recognition of interconnectedness motivates us to serve in the world and brings healing. It serves us all to see ourselves in others. I see myself in you, and therefore I want you to be well. I hope you have that deep level of respect for yourself. I see myself in the planet, so I want the planet to be healthy. Black Elk said, "And while I stood there I saw more than I can tell and I understood more than I saw; for I was seeing in a sacred manner the shapes of all things in the spirit, and the shape of all shapes as they must live together like one being."[4]

Understanding interconnectedness has practical importance. We are interdependent with everything and everyone. The Buddha taught that there is no separate self. In separateness lies the world's greatest misery; in compassion lies the world's true strength. Even our least significant thoughts, words, and actions have consequences throughout the universe. If you throw a pebble into a pond, its ripples create other ripples that create other ripples and other ripples. This is the butterfly effect in which a small change here can result in large differences there. When you purify your heart and mind, the ripple goes out and out and out. A single moment of mindfulness leads to another moment of mindfulness. This universal truth becomes the rallying cry of our practice on behalf of all beings everywhere. It's this truth that motivates the hero and the great bodhisattvas in the world. It's time to take a stand for all life on Earth.

Recognizing interbeing, we cultivate connection and gratitude (and we complain a little less). Interconnectedness is the key to forgiveness. We all come from the same source. We're part of the same tree of life, the Edenic tree of knowledge. George Washington Carver said, "How far you go in life depends on your being tender with the young, compassionate with the aged, sympathetic with the striving, and tolerant of the weak and strong because someday you will have been all of these."[5] We are everything. When we see oneness in all things, we see ourselves in everyone we meet. César Chávez said, "We cannot seek achievement for ourselves and forget about progress and prosperity for our community.... Our ambitions must be broad enough to include the aspirations and needs of others, for their sake and for our own."

The Dalai Lama writes, "No matter what is going on around you, never give up. Develop the heart. Too much energy is spent in your country on developing the mind instead of the heart. Be compassionate, not just to your friends, but to everyone. Work for peace in your heart and in the world.... Never give up."[6] It's your life, and you can choose how you want to live it. To some degree, we all have traumatic stress. Like fallen angels, we've lost the use of our wings, and it's time for us to regain them so we can take flight. One wing is compassion and the other is wisdom. These wings work together to carry us further and further on our journey. To fly, we need both. Wisdom helps us see and accept the truths of life. Wisdom and compassion are the wings of awakening, our protectors.

Our outrage, concern, and despair are an expression of how much we love, and so we can turn it into a powerful form of compassion, the kind of compassion Dr. King, Nelson Mandela, César Chavez, Steven Biko, Black Elk, Gandhi, Wangari Maathai, Malala Yousafzai and so many others had and have. They are standing with us. Stay close to your soul tribe and unite in the light of truth. There's work to do. Hold your head high, and don't give in to despair. The Truth is stronger than a lie. Pens, poster boards and picket signs are just the beginning. Do what's right, and resist what isn't. Dr. King said, "If you can't fly, then run. If you can't run, then walk. If you can't walk, then crawl. But whatever you do, you have to keep moving forward."[7]

We each carry within our hearts what is needed for the healing of our world at this time. It's the gift you came here to bring, and you will find your unique way to express it. Trust your innermost being, trust in your true nature. My prayers are that you find your call to action. In spite of this world breaking my heart over and over, I love it with every ounce of my being. I signed on as a friend and I hope that you do too. If you ever get lost, look at the path closely, then ask yourself, one question: Does this path have heart? If it does, then follow it, friend.

**My Closing Prayer**

For the benefit of all beings and for all life on earth,
Please Stand Up.

For the seven generations from now, Please Stand Up.

For our Ancestors and all those who have come before
us I ask you to Please Stand Up.

For all those without a voice, abused, lost, and neglected
I ask you to Please Stand Up.

For the indigenous Earth keepers and protectors I ask you
to Please Stand Up.

For all those who have died defending the sacred I ask
you to Please Stand Up.

In the name of wisdom and infinite compassion, together
with a Fierce Heart, we will Stand Up.

# NOTES

## CHAPTER 1

1. "The Journey" from *Dream Work* by Mary Oliver. Copyright © 1986 by Mary Oliver. Used by permission of Grove/Atlantic, Inc.

## CHAPTER 3

Epigraph: Jarvis Jay Masters, *Finding Freedom: Writings from Death Row* (Junction City, CA: Padma Publishing), pg. 111

1. A bodhisattva is an awakened being who commits their life to helping others awaken.

2. The Jata Sutta, Samyutta Nikaya 7.6.

3. "Redemption Song" by Bob Marley from *Uprising* by Bob Marley and the Wailers, Island Records, 1980.

## CHAPTER 4

Epigraph: Paraphrase of the Dhammapada, XX, verse 4: "You, yourselves, must walk the path. Buddhas only show the way."

1. From "To Build a Swing," in Hafiz, *The Gift* (New York: Penguin Compass, 1999).

2. http://newbeginningsprayer.org/reflections_-_thomas_merton.

3. Kahlil Gibran, *The Prophet* (New York: Alfred A. Knopf, 1923).

4. From the Assu Sutta, Samyutta Nikaya 15.3. *Samsara* is a Sanskrit and Pali word meaning "wandering." It refers to the endless round of suffering, much of which we create for ourselves.

## CHAPTER 5

1. From The Tibetan Book of the Dead.

2. From an address to the Commonwealth Club, San Francisco, November 9, 1984.

3. Lorna Kelly, *The Camel Knows the Way* (self-published, 2004).

## CHAPTER 6

Epigraph: Wendell Berry, "To Know the Dark," from *The Selected Poems of Wendell Berry* (Berkeley: Counterpoint Press, 1999).

1. Elaine Pagels, *The Gnostic Gospels* (New York: Random House, 1979).

2. Jack Kornfield, *Buddha's Little Instruction Book* (New York: Bantam, 1994).

## CHAPTER 7

Epigraph: Thich Nhat Hanh, *The Path of Emancipation*, (Berkeley: Parallax Press, 2000).

1. From Jennifer Welwood, *Poems for the Path* (self-published).

## CHAPTER 9

Epigraph: Often attributed to Aboriginal elder Lilla Watson, she has asked that it be attributed to the 'Aboriginal Activist Group, Queensland, 1975.' See http://unnecessaryevils.blogspot.com/2008/11/attributing-words.html

1. His Holiness the Dalai Lama, *The Art of Happiness: A Handbook for Living* (New York: Riverhead Books, 2009).

2. Jack Canfield and Mark Victor Hansen, *A Third Serving of Chicken Soup for the Soul* (Deerfield Beach, FL: Health Communications, Inc., 1996).

3. The Four Noble Truths are the Buddha's basic teaching on suffering and on the transformation of suffering by way of the Noble Eightfold Path.

## CHAPTER 10

1. Ajahn Chah, *The Collected Teachings of Ajahn Chah* (Chennai, India: Aruna Publications, 2011).

2. Pema Chödrön, *The Places that Scare You: A Guide to Fearlessness in Difficult Times* (Boulder, CO: Shambhala Publications, 2002).

3. Jarvis Jay Masters, *Finding Freedom: Writings from Death Row* (Junction City, CA: Padma Publishing, 1997).

4. From Jennifer Welwood, *Poems for the Path* (self-published).

## CHAPTER 11

Epigraph: While Nelson Mandela has used this quote, its original source is unclear. http://blogs.shu.edu/diplomacyresearch/2013/12/11/an-exemplar-of-forgiving-prisoner-nelson-mandela/

1. The Plan of Delano, 1966. http://chavez.cde.ca.gov/ModelCurriculum/Public/Justice.aspx.

2. Eknath Easwaran paraphrasing the Buddha in Eknath Easwaran, *To Love Is to Know Me: The Bhagavad Gita for Daily Living (Vol. 3)* (Tomales, CA: Nilgiri Press, 1993).

3. For more on Bryon Widner, see the documentary *Erasing Hate*, MSNBC, 2011.

4. The Dhammapada, I, verse 5.

## CHAPTER 12

Epigraph: Eduardo Galeano, *Mirrors: Stories of Almost Everyone* (New York: Nation Books, 2010).

1. Satipatthana Sutta, Majjhima Nikaya 10.

2. *Life Magazine*, June 1996; *Reader's Digest*, May 1996.

3. Thich Nhat Hanh, *The Long Road Turns to Joy* (Berkeley, CA: Parallax Press, 2011).

4. Herbert Benson, MD, *The Relaxation Response* (New York: William Morrow, 2000).

## CHAPTER 13

1. A. J. Arberry, *Mystical Poems of Rumi*, poem 112 (Chicago, Il: University of Chicago Press, 1968).

2. The Fourteenth Dalai Lama, ˙ *Kindness, Clarity, and Insight* (Boulder, CO: Shambhala, 1984, 2013).

3. Sedaka Sutta, Samyutta Nikaya 47:19.

4. Derek Walcott, *Collected Poems, 1948–1984* (New York: Farrar, Straus and Giroux, 1987).

## CHAPTER 14

Epigraph: Martin Luther King Jr., "Nonviolence: The Only Road to Freedom," *Ebony Magazine*, 1966.

1. Alice Calaprice, *The New Quotable Einstein* (Princeton, NJ: Princeton University Press 2005).

2. According to Wiktionary, accessed July 19th, 2017, "From Kiowa *aho* ("thank you"), and loaned to many other Native American languages during the 20th century because it was frequently heard at pow-wows and widely used in the Native American Church (NAC)." https://en.wiktionary.org/wiki/aho.

## CHAPTER 15

1. See Jack Kornfield, *The Art of Forgiveness, Lovingkindness, and Peace* (New York: Bantam, 2008).

2. Lotus Sutra, chapter 7.

3. Popularly paraphrased like this, from Margaret Meade, *Continuities in Cultural Evolution* (Oxford and New York: Routledge, 1999).

4. Gandhi's Prayer for Peace, Jean-Pierre Isbouts, *Ten Prayers that Changed the World* (Washington D.C.: National Geographic, 2016).

5. Upaddha Sutta, Samyutta Nikaya 45.2.

6. Martin Luther King Jr., from "Advice for the Living" in Chicago, Il, November 1957, *The Papers of Martin Luther King, Jr., volume IV* (Berkeley: University of California Press, 2000.)

## CHAPTER 16

1. Adapted from Shantideva, Bodhicaryavatara (The Bodhisattva Way of Life), chapter 3.

2. http://www.joannamacy.net/engaged-buddhism/225-learning-to-see-each-other.html.

3. Martin Luther King Jr., *Letter from Birmingham Jail* (August, 1963). https://web.cn.edu/kwheeler/documents/Letter_Birmingham_Jail.pdf.

4. John G. Neihardt, *Black Elk Speaks* (Lincoln, NE: Bison Books, 2014).

5. https://www.nps.gov/nr/travel/cultural_diversity/g_washington_carver_historic_site.html.

6. https://sites.google.com/site/capucinehenryredondalailama/never-give-up---dalai-lama.

7. "Keep Moving from this Mountain," Founders Day Address, Spelman College, 10 April 1960: https://swap.stanford.edu/20141218225553/http://mlk-kpp01.stanford.edu/primarydocuments/Vol5/10Apr1960_KeepMovingfromThis-Mountain,AddressatSpelmanCollege.pdf.

## ACKNOWLEDGMENTS

I have so much gratitude and would like to give a special thanks to my beautiful mentors and wise teachers Jack Kornfield and Alice Walker.

I would also like to give a special thank you to Arnie Kotler and Rachel Neumann, who helped me find my voice and my courage.

I am especially grateful for his Holiness the Dalai Lama, whose loving heart has been my never ending source of strength, wisdom, and courage.

Last, but never least, I would like to thank all those whom I have met and worked with at East Bay Meditation Center. May our light continue to shine for many years to come.

# ABOUT THE AUTHOR

Spring Washam is a well-known meditation and dharma teacher based in Oakland, California. She is a founding member and core teacher at the East Bay Meditation Center located in downtown Oakland. She is the founder of Lotus Vine Journeys, an organization that blends indigenous healing practices with Buddhist wisdom. She was trained by Jack Kornfield and has studied numerous meditation practices and Buddhist philosophy since 1997. She is also a member of the Spirit Rock Teachers Council. In addition to being a teacher, she is also a healer, facilitator, spiritual activist, and writer. She has practiced and studied under some of the most preeminent meditation masters in both the Theravada and Tibetan schools of Buddhism. She has studied indigenous healing practices and works with students individually from around the world. Spring is considered a pioneer in bringing mindfulness based healing practices into diverse communities. She currently travels and teaches workshops, classes, and retreats worldwide.

## RELATED TITLES

*Awakening Joy,* James Baraz and Shoshana Alexander

*Friendship as Freedom,* Kate Johnson

*Healing,* Sister Dang Nghiem

*Learning True Love,* Sister Chan Khong

*No Mud No Lotus,* Thich Nhat Hanh

*Together We Are One,* Thich Nhat Hanh